Love to
Gal Pat.

Mind how you go.

Keith Skipp

1999

The squit and wisdom
of Keith Skipper

Skipper's Byways

Eastern Daily Press

Copyright 1998 Eastern Counties Newspapers

Published by Eastern Counties Newspapers, Prospect House, Rouen Road, Norwich, Norfolk, NR1 1RE.

Printed and bound by Page Bros, Mile Cross Lane, Norwich.

All rights reserved. No part of this publication may be reproduced, stored in a retrieval system, or transmitted, in any form or by any means, electronic, mechanical, photocopying, recording or otherwise, without the prior permission of the publishers.

ISBN 0-9502952-9-9

Produced by Peter Waters.

Photography by Sam Robbins.

FOREWORD

I embarked on my "new" Norfolk voyage in 1987 after being asked to contribute weekly articles to the Eastern Daily Press.

This selection represents just a few stops along the way with Skipper's Log, The Norfolk File and, in more recent times, Skipper's Byways.

As befits a proud native of the best county of them all, I have veered strongly towards subjects close to my heart – durable dialect, rustic humour, village life, farming changes, sporting episodes and childhood yarns.

There are heartfelt salutes towards a few outstanding characters encountered over the years, including my grammar school history master, an old-fashioned policeman and a rural Katharine Hepburn who kept bees and rode a sit-up-and-beg bicycle.

I own up to masquerading as royalty at Wembley on the day the Canaries soared to cup success, and reveal the true facts behind the near-demise of a budgie called Colin.

A plea for Breckland's soul, an anguished cry in the face of wanton vandalism on the coast and the battle to keep community spirit alive in larger villages are among more serious themes on parade.

Several amusing Norfolk stories featured come from EDP readers, while little literary extracts underline my deep affection for local books and writers.

My warmest thanks to many old friends who help keep the local presses rolling, especially those with responsibility for decking out my parochial pulpit over the past decade or so.

I am grateful to Philip Preston and Peter Waters for their enthusiastic backing of this venture. I reserve the biggest bouquet for my wife Diane. Her technological dexterity has transferred Norfolk pride from homely byways to the information highway.

Keith Skipper
Cromer, 1998

Norfolk

It may not be mountain-ribbed like your county, gentle reader; you may scorn it because it has no majestic crags or roaring, rushing torrents, or mighty moors that stretch in wild and eerie solitude; but there is something extremely picturesque and warm in the bright red farms and outhouses peeping slyly from groups of elm or poplar or willow trees, in a bit of good Norfolk valley scenery. A windmill here and there adds quaintness; the river, bulrush and reed-bound, winds like a serpent through the marshes, and reflects in its translucent depths the clear, blue sky above; and the saucy wherries with broad bows and large black sails, with big-trousered and blue-jerseyed watermen, whose humour, like their sailing, is unique, making it impossible for anyone to adjudicate upon the beauty of Norfolk as a comparative thing, but they compel the observer to admit that the county must be allowed to stand on its own distinctive merits pure and simple.

Where The Birds Sing, Charles Roper, 1894

Contents

I was there for our golden age 11
Pushy Mrs Wigham 13
Good-natured greetings asking for a chat 14
Under house arrest on bonfire night 16
Goodbye Uncle Harry, butcher with bible 19
Sporting master of the old school 21
Swaffham treasures 24
Dry observations 25
Parish partners 26
Rural queen of bees and blackberries 27
The secret diary of Hadrian Mule 29
Pulpit feeling 32
Boring mud can stick 33
Past – or future? 34
King-sized ambitions can come true 35
Year grows ripe with that old romance 37
Dale to rescue 40
A belated plea for Breckland's soul 41
Chuckles with Charlie 44
Chalky caterpillars 44
That's Salle 45
Proper hopes 45
The genuine article 46
The day we met null and void 47
True facts about our feathered friend 50
Let's meet farmer on his own midden 53
Give yourself a bit of stick! 56
Bill spoke my language 59
Fowl play led to dibble disaster 61
Beyond the pail with Wally 63
Rustic rib-ticklers in Coronation Milk 65
Pier's the place for Cromer pride 67
Yanks for all the memories 69

P.C. Brian – lighthouse of the law 71
Nostalgia rules..73
Hedgerow harvest 74
Little Troshing set to slay dragons...75
Over the border a sound idea...77
Make a noise to protect peace..79
Heart under strain 81
Size need not kill village spirit..83
The old quest for a straight furrow 85
Squit on internet 87
Sporting reunion 88
Squit with chain gang...90
King Arthur holds court at Trunch 91
Little Troshing has time on hands 93
Grave mistake 96
Professor of dialect...97
Taking Dickey out of old customs 99
Finding the way..102
Past and future unite 103
Golden day ruined by wrecked seat 105
Countryside custodians 107
Little Troshing's cover-up plan..109

Norfolk salute to St.George 111

Books ends..113

Epilogue...119

I WAS THERE FOR OUR GOLDEN AGE

All too often I am asked to justify my glowing references to Norfolk's most recent Golden Age – the 1950s. Frankly, I find it easier to pile on the praise as the years roll by.

Yes, distance lends enchantment, and a country childhood has been known to inspire natural affection. I suspect the decade earning my laurels is about to become very fashionable.

However, it goes much deeper than that. I have arrived at the time of comparisons, and I'm bound to take the 1950s as my yardstick. Some of those comparisons are odious, but I can't help smiling as I hear echoes of distant grown-up voices in "Now, when I was young" sermons scattered across a much-changed landscape.

I can proffer a number of solid reasons why the Norfolk of over 40 years ago tops the favourites' list. It was a time of rebuilding after the war, both in family and community. People were glad to see each other, and they showed it.

After the Festival of Britain came the Coronation to stretch rural ambitions with a crop of village signs, village halls and village playing fields. The decade came to a climax with that memorable Norwich City FA Cup run to the semi-finals. Don't scoff – it remains one of the most passionate episodes in many people's lives.

I was at school throughout the whole ten years, and didn't stay in once to write a hundred times: "I must be prepared for dual carriageways and diversification in farming."

Life was much quieter, much slower, much more straightforward. I know because I was there, growing up in a village where a commuter was a rarity. The school, with no threat of closure, was at the heart of the place, passing on the fundamentals with plenty of affection and few trimmings.

Chapel, church, pub, village hall, shop, green, war memorial, aerodrome... we weren't short of essential items that made up the country jigsaw of the time.

Aerodrome? Oh yes, Beeston sort of shared that with Wendling, and you'll never guess what sort of wings dominate the scene there these days. Give in? I'm talking turkey.

Sergeants' Mess and Water Tower Site really were in Beeston, and I think often how easy it would have been for a kind of "rustic apartheid" to have operated in the village when I was a lad.

Small concrete huts, huddled together in a gradual dilapidation since the early war years, made up the Beeston Drome settlement. The long struggle to rehouse tenants did not end until 1963 when the last family left for a council house at North Elmham.

Perhaps a few "true villagers" resented the automatic connection between Beeston and the Drome, with its "problem families". Even so, my main impression carried over from the days when the huts provided homes for a fair number of our local population is of a genial tolerance on one side – and a reasonably cheerful forebearance on the other.

All right, we don't deserve badges, but it must be worth pointing to a rough-and-ready harmony always on the books at Beeston school. Testament, surely, to the wise counsel of our teachers and parents. Children can be cruel, and they get the idea and the mood behind it from their seniors. If the example is better, so is behaviour at playground level.

Let me list some of the "traditional" images of village life as paraded by Beeston & Co. of the 1950s in the hope of prompting a few nods of recognition...

Evangelists in a tent on a meadow full of buttercups; Americans marching on Remembrance Sunday; Friday night pictures in the Nissen hut village hall; Sunday school anniversary and outing; carol singing with a tilley lamp up front; chapel preacher for tea; tradesmen at the front door; ration books at the shop; the "Nit Nurse" inspecting little shocks of hair...

Cuttings from a village scrapbook. A Norfolk village. Then there were things harder to put into words...

The way elders of the parish gave you the time of day. You had to earn their special favours, gap-toothed smiles under the cap or bonnet, with an apprenticeship in being polite as a matter of course. Come the day when you were saluted first. They saw something in you, and you were so glad your respect was genuine.

The way school became much more than a place to read books and write compositions. Suddenly, you noticed he could do country dancing like a dream even though his trousers were ragged and his hobnail boots were all scuffed up.

The way girls looked through you as you ached on the other side of the dancing dervishes on big nights at the village hall. Please let her ask me for a waltz! Please let her embarrass someone else!

The way the same gramaphone records blared across the

bowling-for-the-pig contingent at the village fete. Why didn't they organise a play-off between Frankie Laine, Guy Mitchell, Jo Stafford, Johnny Ray, Lita Roza, Dickie Valentine, David Whitfield, Doris Day, Winifred Atwell and her other piano, Eddie Fisher, The Stargazers and Petula Clark?

The way you knew deep down they wouldn't believe you all those years later when you extolled the simple virtues of a golden era. We are not the first to be disbelieved, patronised, ignored, mocked or told to stop wallowing in silly old nostalgia.

But we might be the last.

PUSHY MRS WIGHAM

August was doing its best to pluck a day from high November as we left Swaffham's sprawl behind and found legions of trees standing guard over countryside.

Unseasonable squalls had put harvest on hold under grumpy skies. Half-cut fields waited for sun. Dark puddles marked the road through Cockley Cley.

We looked in vain for Iceni warriors sheltering beneath giant branches railing against such unlikely blasts. Despite the weather, Oxburgh Hall extended a warm welcome and exuded an air of timeless serenity.

"Been here since the 1480s, and this is my first visit," I said with a tinge of guilt. Always the same, glories on your doorstep have to wait. Another shower carried on a boisterous wind smacked me in the face as if in mock punishment.

A war-like muster of gatehouse, towers and battlements reflected in a moat satisfied any immediate thoughts of medieval marauders being kept at bay. But an altogether more mellow mood took hold as we savoured the beauties of the Bedingfield family home.

The boys voted the priest hole most interesting item. They scrambled inside and imagined themselves being hunted. We told them a little about religious intolerance without making it sound too much like a lecture.

My wife gasped in admiration at handiwork in the tapestry room. Displayed flat under glass in a controlled light to preserve them and to show them to best advantage, these intricate embroideries were made in the 1500s by Mary, Queen of Scots and Elizabeth, Countess of Shrewsbury, two of the finest needlewomen of their day.

I was intrigued by a portrait on the stairs of a woman bearing an uncanny resemblance to Nora Batty. A mixture of severity, domesticity and "cross me at your peril!" under a bonnet.

I discovered it was Mrs Wigham, the Fourth Baronet's housekeeper. One of her main duties was to push his lordship around in the 18th century invalid's chair on display.

Fear of heights encouraged me to decline the offer of some wonderful views from the roof. Gardens, woods and walks carry far more appeal at ground level, especially when there is half a gale blowing and rain needling in at all angles.

"We'll come back in November when the weather's better," I said as we left this compelling spot, avoiding the obvious temptation to make a bad joke about the National Rust.

The boys are bound to enjoy a few more lows and highs of history. The wife can take one of her tapestries to compare notes with Mary, Queen of Scots.

I'll just keep my feet on the ground – and stay out of Mrs Wigham's way. She looks the pushy sort.

GOOD-NATURED GREETINGS ASKING FOR A CHAT

One of the key reasons for preserving remnants of the local dialect is to ensure some variety in our hails and farewells.

The grudging "g'morning" and the dismissive "g'bye", bookends of today, compare miserably with the sparkling banter we shared not so long ago.

I can hear the expected chorus: "Here he goes again... dispensing romantic twaddle about the past." But if you have been about for three decades or more, just listen now to some of the voices crowding in with little reminders.

For me, they are a lasting legacy of a country upbringing at a time when communication was more of a straightforward business.

Yes, you really did know everyone in the village and most folk in the immediate area. It was automatic to make some kind of verbal contact when you met.

The very least on offer was the seal of the day, a casual nod and mimed greeting as you passed. Usually held back for newcomers yet to make an impact on the community, or your darts colleague who had let you down on double 13 the night before.

Complete strangers invariably collected a forceful "Hent sin yew round these parts afore, ole partner", just to make them feel reasonably at home or to put them on their guard if intentions were not entirely reasonable. The hand of friendship with one admonishing finger at the ready – like so many Norfolk expressions.

So, let us line up a few good old Norfolk greetings, worthy of much more than a nostalgic sigh as we battle across the plains of indifference to the mountain range of anti-social antics inspired by the likes of the personal stereo.

The majority of these time-honoured hellos demand better than a half-hearted grunt in reply:

"How yer gittin' on?", "Wodyer say, then?", "How yer blowin', ole partner?", "Nyce ter see yer, my bewty!", "Cor blarst, is that really yew lookin' ser well?", "Dun't tell me – yew're lorst a tanner an' fownd thrippence!", "I kin see a lyte on – but is ennywun at hoom?", "Fanser bumpin' itter yew arter orl this tyme!", "I thowt yew'd emigrearted!", "They towld me yew wuz ded!".

Good-natured inquiries asking for a chat. They flourished before our lives became digital and dynamic, before getting from A to B became simply a matter of speed rather than a chance to enjoy a mardle.

Of course, far more people strolled and biked when I was a lad in the country, and the general pace encouraged amiable encounters all along the way.

A walk round the village after chapel on Sunday evening was perfect preparation for the rigours of a new week. It brought reassurances with regular sights and sounds.

If those good-natured inquiries so often built a springboard for spontaneous rustic drollery, the looks that went with them were worthy of any top-of-the-bill comic mixing pathos with punchy one-liners.

I saw and studied those faces inspire music-hall items in the harvest field when we stopped for refreshment and in the barn when the rain needled down.

Laughter didn't always come easy to a boy on the sidelines, but that was the beauty of such diversions; instant examinations in the classroom on the farm.

The richness and variety of swift responses to Norfolk-sized greetings never ceases to amaze or amuse, even though give-and-take sessions are less fashionable these days.

Listen very carefully, and you may still hear "Batterannerhebbin" and "Wassanwotterwuz", with old favourite "Fair ter middlin'" sandwiched in between.

"Nut tew bad", "Tell yer the trewth, I dun't fare no matters terday", "Werry sadly", "Still on the ground, jammin' bowt!", "Carn't cumplearn, an' that wunt dew no good ennyhow", "My skull feel thow that berlong ter sumwun else, and they're welcome tew it!", " I ent long fer this wald – so buy us a pynt!"

All right. These may not be in the Shakespeare class. "Ill met by moonlight, proud Titania" and "Parting is such sweet sorrow" have obvious qualities.

But when did the old Bard come anywhere near The Boy John, alias Sidney Grapes, when he uttered or wrote those immortal words: "Well, fare yer well tergether!"

I still prefer that to "Have a nice day!", "BFN – Bye For Now!" or even "Stand not upon the order of your going, but go at once."

I suspect Lady Macbeth was trying to say: "Now cleer yew orff, and mynd how yew go!"

UNDER HOUSE ARREST ON BONFIRE NIGHT

November doesn't have much of a fan club. I suppose we have to accept it as the gateway to winter, with darkness creeping up long before teatime and cold, grey hands stretching out in the mornings.

After Bonfire Night, youngsters have their impatience fed for the next big fling by weeks of television teasing and high street enticing. The gap between fireworks and presents under the bed still assumes nightmare proportions for some children.

November is an indoor month. As John Clare put it in his Shepherd's Calendar... "day seems turned to night and trys to wake in vain". The ideal time, then, to catch up with some of the books picked up during the summer.

I recall one Guy Fawkes night over 40 years ago when reading didn't come easy through a flood of tears. The memory still stings every time I hear a Little Demon burst its lungs or spy a rocket trailing stars.

It had been a busy and productive half-term holiday. My mate Tubby Rye persuaded his dad to let us have some old tyres out of the barn to provide the perfect bed for the bonfire.

We caressed them into the middle of the meadow, a sensible distance from the hut where plans had been hatched to circumnavigate the world when we left school – without girls – and to form Beeston's first millionaire skiffle group. Then we'd have all the female company we could handle.

The tyres waited for trimmings. We even put our best-of-320 cricket match series on ice for a few hours in favour of hauling branches and brambles to the pyre. It began to rise like a wigwam without the proper planning requirements.

A lively overnight breeze found the village knee-deep in leaves the next morning. We wanted our share of November's bounty, and Tubby's wobbly old cart could now come into its own in the haulage business. Dinner went by the board as we brushed and scooped up and down the road, urging the cart to take just one more armful before we coaxed it to the growing mound on the meadow.

At least 50 trips later, we yielded to hunger and darkness. With a small prayer to the gods who look after bonfires before they're supposed to go up in smoke – "Please, don't let it rain!" – I raced home. The best we'd ever built, and how the pride would shine on our faces tomorrow night as flames leapt high into the sky.

My big mistake was to wear my new rubber boots for the final preparations. Perhaps I wanted to look more like a real worker after several lectures from village worthies about lack of size and ability letting me down on this score.

Black and shiny, and obviously expensive, they gave me that touch of rural class. Tubby was impressed, and said I could tidy up that bit on the other side where the brambles were wandering.

For just about the first time in my young life, I put some beef into a manual task. I soon realised it would be sheer folly ever to do it again. The pitchfork sliced into my left boot, leaving it mortally injured. A gaping hole screamed at me, but I couldn't answer back. Tubby's mum had baled me out countless times, with cotton and thread, soap and water, turpentine and plasters. But this one was beyond her tender mercies. I feared the worst, and it came after a sullen tea and a blubbering confession.

With no apparent concern for the possible consequences of their actions – my development as a useful member of society could have been set back at least a term or two – my parents decreed it would be best if I stayed indoors for the duration of these Guy Fawkes celebrations.

I sobbed at the unfairness of it all. Others reaping the benefits of my half-term harvest! Brothers and sisters out on the illuminated trail while I sat in front of the grate like Cinderella in overalls, trying to find some consolation in "Treasure Island" and a crackling wireless!

For one mad moment I thought about making a dash for it, hurling the rubber boots on the bonfire, along with the offending pitchfork and dancing barefoot around the sizzling tyres and crackling brambles. The thought of a clip round the ear in front of all those people pulled me back from the brink of insanity...

That night of confinement – house arrest, if you like – haunts me every year about this time. That hole in the rubber boot left a yawning gap in my social calendar. I had to wait another seven weeks for an old man to struggle down the chimney to leave black and shiny boots under the bed.

Mind you, they came as a bit of a surprise after those escapades involving pancakes on the kitchen lightshade and home-made toffee in the old wind-up gramophone.

I suspect the old boy with a beard, and black boots, is more sympathetic to tears than a plotter pitchforked to fame by gunpowder.

***

THEY DEW SAY
Horry: How dew yew manage ter save any munny these days?
Tom: Oh, I cut down on them lectrisity bills.
Horry: An' how dew yew dew that, ole partner?
Tom: For a start, only plug the lectric clock in when I want ter know the time!

GOODBYE UNCLE HARRY, BUTCHER WITH BIBLE

Uncle Harry's funeral couldn't be too sombre an occasion. He soared above sadness so many times with that powerful voice and simple faith during his 69 years that we felt obliged to bid farewell with good tunes rather than January tears.

We sang The Old Rugged Cross and Safe In The Arms of Jesus with anxious gusto, as if it was only a matter of time before his ringing tones put our best efforts to shame. But we wanted to show willing.

Harry John Wyett, master butcher and masterful preacher, was buried in the churchyard at Thornham under heavy skies. The service, blessed with a packed congregation inside and relayed to many others outside, was held in the cosy Methodist chapel next door.

The chapel is directly opposite the butcher's shop where Harry ran his village business for 25 years. Customers lined the street, exchanging stories about this man, engaging and energetic, who was never frightened to mix the bible with business.

Harry delivered a little sermon with the sausages, a text with the topside, if he felt it would do some good. Infectiously cheerful, he could not believe that a striped apron and straw boater out of the Corporal Jones wardrobe could hamper his recruitment drive for God's Army.

Religion wasn't something to be hauled out like a well-creased suit on a Sunday. Harry's enthusiasm simply came to a peak as he exchanged the shop counter and delivery basket for the hymn book and the pulpit.

An extrovert nature – hardly a family trait – made him a popular choice for harvest festivals and Sunday school anniversaries. "That bloke what smile a lot and sing loud" – the sort of testimonial he loved from the time a trade bike was an essential part of the meat business.

Harry picked up the trade and the bike in Beeston, the mid-Norfolk village where his mother May (my dear old Nanna) did so much to make the chapel an essential part of country life. He served his butchery apprenticeship just a few yards up the road from the chapel at Ted Margarson's village stores.

Other chapel stalwarts like Walter Ward and Harry Dawson were early inspirations as he joined the preaching rounds. The meat business took him on to Brancaster, Sedgeford and, finally, Thornham.

At his peak, Harry served 10 villages from his Sedgeford shop, and delivered to Sculthorpe airbase as well. I can't swear it was deliberate – Norfolk people like to leave you guessing – but I heard him described once as a butcher "full of evangelical veal."

His twinkling sense of humour, coupled with an endless supply of Norfolk character sketches, many of them drawn over a cup of tea on delivery day, made him easy to listen to, whether he was in the back kitchen or the pulpit.

Harry sang with pace and power, dictating to the organist and lifting the congregation with him. When he let rip, a few chapel ceilings must have felt like surrendering!

My affection for him turned to near-idolatry in 1955 when, on hearing I had passed the 11-plus, he invited me to Sedgeford for a holiday before I got down to business at grammar school.

It was my first time away from the old Beeston homestead, and Sedgeford might as well have been Sacramento or Singapore as I blubbered myself to sleep the first night. No reflection on Harry, Aunt Amy or cousins Billy, Paul and Mark... I still have trouble coming to terms with being uprooted from my familiar environment and routine.

On that first holiday I saw Uncle Harry's style at first hand. Every customer in the shop was made to feel special. Every trek up the garden path to deliver a joint was the start of a little adventure.

Such enthusiasm kept Harry going as a family butcher until his retirement a year ago. In some ways, his role as a hospital visitor replaced those regular missions round the houses. He needed people, he relished company – and he stayed true to the "old fashioned" chapel preaching style.

His funeral was a thanksgiving, a Norfolk village salute from family and friends. It was with no sense of guilt that we shared anecdotes and laughs over cups of tea and sausage rolls.

Cousin Billy set the mood with his yarn about Harry plucking a chicken while pedalling the old trade bike in gale-force winds at Brancaster. Not the only time he made the feathers fly!

SPORTING MASTER OF
THE OLD SCHOOL

Mr Dimock was surprisingly vague on his dates.

He had been chairman for "several years", but his election in the first place was "something of an accident" because of a misunderstanding over when and where the meeting should be held.

Typically modest, I mused. Playing down his role as a key figure in the improved fortunes of Swaffham Cricket Club. But I did anticipate more respect for specific dates.

Geoffrey Dimock taught history at Hamond's in the town for 24 years (1950 – 1974). He was instrumental in my grammar school education taking a dramatic U-turn after the summer holidays of 1960.

With four O-levels and no job, I returned to the old seat of learning, heartily sick of bean-picking and penetrating questions about plans for the future.

Mr Dimock took compassion on the waif-like character looking for something to happen outside one of his classes. With his backing, I was put on probation in the sixth form.

I rewarded Mr Dimock's faith by taking history along with English, and tested his staying power with essays three or four times longer than anyone else's. He recalled those long-winded efforts as we chatted in Swaffham Assembly Rooms, the setting for our school dinners when he was master and I was pupil.

My revenge was two-fold. I recalled the number of times meaningful discussion about the treaty of Utrecht or the Seven Years' War had been delayed in his lessons.

"Thought Crossan had a good game Saturday, sir" or "Do you reckon Laker is over the hill yet, sir?" were perfect ploys to eat up a useful part of the history period with current sporting affairs.

My second course was even sweeter. He had to be quiet and listen to me, dispensing the sort of eulogy popular schoolteachers used to endure when Robert Donat was waving goodbye to the likes of Mr Chips.

A few weeks ago, Swaffham Cricket Club played their way into the First Division of the Norfolk League, and won the Stan Biss Vase, a Sunday competition. Fitting achievements in their bicentenary year. I resist the obvious temptation to infer that Mr Dimock featured in their earliest fixtures.

The celebration dance ground to a respectful halt as I made presentations to him and two other club stalwarts, Ronnie Howard and Billy Shingfield.

Mr Dimock collected a golf bag, a clear indication that present sporting feats bowl along at a more sedate pace. Mind you, after so many seasons of taking wickets, scoring runs and talking his colleagues through them, golf has reminded him how the smaller ball can be even more dangerous.

He was struck a glancing blow on the side of the head not long ago, "but I carried on after getting to my feet and discovering I wasn't dead."

Mr Dimock – it's still impossible to call him Geoffrey, even after all these years – invited me to play in his farewell cricket match when he retired from the school in 1974.

We enjoyed a good mardle then, and picked up the threads the other evening as he apologised profusely to my wife for being partly responsible for what she is lumbered with today. Nothing patronising about my old history master.

We mulled over the Canary Cup Run of 1958-59, as if by talking about it we might inspire something similar to stir local passions during the next few months.

He remembered how he got tickets for certain ties, the friendships forged out of memorable combat, the way Luton stole Norwich City's passport to Wembley...

I remembered how the Dimock household played host to a select band of school cricket enthusiasts during many a dinner hour when the Pedlar Cafe, frothy coffee and the Shadows' latest hit on the jukebox did not call.

"Wonderful Land" was often a cup of tea and a grandstand seat in front of the television for Test match action.

As a small token of my appreciation Mr Dimock let me hand in this little bit of history homework to coincide with the club's bicentenary celebrations, and as a salute to "your years at the helm".

There are indications that Swaffham were playing cricket in 1769, and finding it hard to work up a good sporting relationship with Shipdham; reasons for the animosity are still being explored.

However, Swaffham take 1788 as the "official" starting point, with a match against Northwold which they won. The clubs still meet, although no stake money is involved.

That curtain-raiser with Northwold came a year after the American Constitution was drafted, and a year before George

Washington became the first US president, and the French Revolution began. (Shipdham was not connected with the latter event as far as we know.)

In 1788 itself, the MCC issued their first edition of The Laws. Among other matters it cleared up a ruling which until then had allowed strikers to impede the fielding side in certain circumstances.

If we jump a few seasons, to July, 1797, we meet 33 local lads lining up to take on the All-England Eleven at Swaffham, with 500 guineas at stake.

Norfolk could muster only 131 in their two innings – 50 and 81 – while the All-England side made 144 in one innings. So, "the greatest cricket match ever played in Norfolk" saw the big boys defy big odds.

I had not forgotten, Mr Dimock, that the Impeachment of Warren Hastings began in 1788, although I can't remember if he bowled round the wicket to the left-hander when he wasn't looking or failed to hand in his essay on time.

I do know Mr Dimock is worthy of the tribute paid in the booklet produced to celebrate Hamond's 250th anniversary in 1986...

"A well-loved schoolmaster who contributed as much to the informal as the formal education of his pupils. A keen games player, he had a go at most sports, though cricket is probably his favourite. He still symbolises Hamond's for many old boys."

Truly a master of the old school – even if he is vague about some aspects of his career as a cricket club chairman. David Amis, his successor in the post, says Mr Dimock became chairman in 1962.

Now, that's a year he ought to recall with great clarity and delight. I left school – and took my marathon essays with me.

***

THEY DEW SAY
Tom: My missus dunt harf keep a'gittin' on ter me.
Horry: Myne's jist the searme – that creaze yer.
Tom: Dew she moan an' groan bowt evrathing, ole partner?
Horry: That she dew. If I bort a prayin' mantis rekun that'd be the wrong relijun!

SWAFFHAM TREASURES

The Pedlar of Swaffham was ushered towards London Bridge to hear about his pot of gold. I only had to turn up at Swaffham to be presented with some real Norfolk treasures.

I was browsing round the shelves of a second-hand bookshop near the market place when Eric Drake tapped me on the shoulder. He said he and his wife June would like to find a good home for the work of one of the town's outstanding characters this century.

Well, you don't get that sort of offer every Tuesday morning – and I was flattered enough to cut short my shopping expedition and follow Eric home.

His brother Reg, who died a few years ago, was a prolific writer, respected historian and acknowledged expert on John Chapman, the Pedlar who gave a large slice of his fortune to the parish church I got to know well during seven years at the town's grammar school.

In 1982 Reg Drake unearthed evidence to suggest that Chapman, far from being the kindly benefactor with a heart of gold, could have been a conniving blackmailer and a liar. I'll be sifting through the Chapman file and other material to support that argument during the winter months.

Reg penned hundreds of articles, stories, poems and scripts for radio and television, but did not attract the reputation such industry, scholarship and style deserved. I'm particularly fond of his dialect offerings.

His version of the Swaffham Pedlar grips the imagination like this: "Years and dickies a years ago, long afore you and me was born, old John lived in a little old bit of a shant jest orf the market square with Keartie his wife, two titty totty boys, a little old bearby mawther and his dawg..."

Eric and June Drake live and breathe local history in a fascinating home nearly 300 years old. It was built by Robert Godrick in London Street.

He brought Methodism to Swaffham and John Wesley, founder of the movement, twice preached from a bedroom window in the house, the second time in October 1790, six months before he died.

A man fell to his death from the roof of the house in 1775 as he tried to protect the thatch during the Great Fire of Swaffham. It started in the Blue Boar Inn and, fanned by a strong north wind, destroyed 22 properties and badly damaged two more.

My history refresher course continued as I bumped into David Butters, amiable curator of the town's museum. We mardled outside the Assembly Rooms, looking drab and sad despite the sunshine.

David reminded me how the building hosted glittering balls for the local nobility when Swaffham was the social hub of 18th century West Norfolk.

I reminded him how the old place still had a veneer of gracious living as we tucked into our school dinners nearly 40 years ago.

We agreed a modern Pedlar was called for to provide a little pot of gold – and a big pot of paint.

DRY OBSERVATIONS

The Norfolk art of understatement, as highlighted by Dick Bagnall-Oakeley, is well illustrated in this yarn from Chris Basey of North Burlingham

Dick was driving home from Norwich late one night in atrocious weather when he picked out in his headlights a figure walking ahead in the rain. He stopped and said: "You'd better get in here out of the wet."

The chap got into the car and sat there with water pouring from his hat, coat and just about everywhere else.

Not a word was spoken for a considerable time.

Eventually the passenger looked at Dick and said: "Thass a poor dry out ternite, marster."

In the same vein – although this does not come from the Bagnall-Oakeley collection – is the story of two American servicemen who failed to negotiate the A47 bend at Burlingham during the last war.

They ended up in a pit alongside the road. They managed to crawl out, but the car was left upside down in the water.

As they surveyed the sad scene, the local blacksmith arrived and observed dryly:

"One good thing about it – if yew wuz thinking o' dewin' a job on the bottom, now's yor time, ole partners."

PARISH PARTNERS

Byways researchers, always probing for ideas to revive our local community spirit, reckon they are on a winner with a Norfolk village twinning programme.

Find something in common and get on the Parish Partners register. All you need is a map, a sense of humour and a taste for cultural exchanges.

This week' Top 10 features the lucky communities taking part in a pilot project sanctioned by Norfolk Rural Community Council:

1 Baconsthorpe/Egmere
2 Appleton/Syderstone
3 Bale/Wheatacre
4 Herringby/Cranworth
5 Burston/Riddlesworth
6 Rushall/Sloley
7 Swannington/Cobholm
8 Dickleburgh/Whittington
9 Foxley/Wolferton
10 Babingley/Brooke

***

PERFECT TIMING
I like the story of the Norfolk bishop who went to stay overnight with one of his parsons.
The bishop came down to breakfast and was surprised to hear Rock of Ages rising lustily forth from the kitchen. Pleased to imagine that this was an early-morning form of worship, he asked the parson's son to tell him who was singing.
"That's dear old Mabel the cook," the boy replied. "She always sings Rock of Ages when she boils eggs for breakfast. Three verses for soft-boiled and five verses for hard-boiled."

RURAL QUEEN OF BEES
AND BLACKBERRIES

Mildred Symonds spoke softly, kept bees and rode one of those sit-up-and-beg bicycles.

She taught at the Church Sunday School. We were Chapel. That didn't stop her displaying an ecumenical streak when we called at the door with blackberries.

Not once in all my years as a hedgerow raider did she reject my rural overtures. Money was never mentioned. Our dealings were above such things. She cradled the jars packed with fresh pickings, asked about the rest of the family and opened the door to her kitchen.

A dark room, but still cosy, friendly, kept warm by all those plants and bushes leaning on the window. It always reminded me of Sunday tea as she fussed towards the larder and I could hear the kettle humming on the hob and smell the blooms on the sill.

Mildred invariably praised the quality of the fruit, smoothed her pinafore and then, gently, almost furtively, took some coins from her purse.

Sweaty, stained fingers let go of the secret a few yards up the road. I had knocked on the door and asked if she wanted some blackberries. I would share out the bounty.

She was more generous than anyone else in the village. Just occasionally, her husband John would throw an old-fashioned look our way as we trundled up the path. But we won him over when the snows melted and we asked if he could be so kind as to pass on these primroses, cowslips and violets to Mrs Symonds.

She died a few days ago at the age of 97 and was buried in the old village churchyard at Beeston. In her closing years she kept an eye – and an ear – on me from a distance at St Nicholas' Home for the Elderly at Dereham.

I received regular reports from Mr and Mrs Harry Richardson who used to live next door to her at Beeston. They dropped in for a mardle with Mildred when a neighbourly natter over the fence was no longer possible.

Mildred told them a few yarns about those blackberry-flavoured days, and, as far as I know, did nothing to sully my reputation as a mild-mannered lad ready to do a spot of overtime along the autumn lanes.

However, she did take exception to something I said on the

wireless two or three years ago. I was passing on birthday greetings and it seemed reasonable to call her "a grand old lady" in her nineties.

Mildred's niece, Jessie Bowden, told me the other day that auntie was delighted with the birthday wishes but less than pleased with the label.

"She hinted she would give you what for... 'old' indeed!" That ranks alongside a comment from my wife's Great Aunt Bess, who went to a Darby and Joan Club in Gloucester when she was 86. Asked what it was like, she snapped: "I'm not going there again – it's full of old fogies!"

MIldred Symonds, born in Beeston in 1891, got up early to tend her garden. Many a morning as I passed on the way to school, she would look up and use a hoe or fork to wave a greeting. And she'd be there still as I raced home to organise a cricket epic on the orchard pitch because news had come through that Tubby Rye was prepared to travel with his bat.

A dash to the shop before tea would find Mildred organising a gentle retreat. The only time she gave cause for concern was when she donned that strange hat-and-veil outfit to attend to her beehives.

A rural Katherine Hepburn looking for her African Queen and we were scared enough to run by without the customary exchange as strange noises seeped through the foliage.

Honey, jam, bottled fruit, flowers, plants, vegetables, pleasantries... she dispensed them all with the same gentle, unhurried manner that characterised her cycling to the church or the Rectory Room.

In so many memorable ways, she represented the solid, dependable and unchanging face of village life. Always there as we went to and fro, gathering pace and anxious to grow up and look over bigger hedges.

Then, years later, we are so grateful for those little bridges back into the past. Even as I reflected on Mildred's cottage industries, and the way they enhanced harvest festivals and other village events, a letter came from Sleaford.

Retired schoolteacher Joan Waite recalled holidays in Beeston with aunt and uncle, Mary and Bob Hall. Ah, yes – I remember them well! Joan and her sister, Hilary, often walked to Litcham... but always ran past a turkey farm on the way in case one had escaped!

Suddenly, I didn't feel so guilty about belting past the Symonds' household when the bees were making angry noises.

THE SECRET DIARY OF HADRIAN MULE

A remarkable document has come to light after gathering dust in a Norfolk attic for much of this century.

The random reflections of a countryman provide a rare insight into local life before the first world war. They were hard times, the workhouse casting a constant shadow, but this cottager-scribe paints them with as much rustic joy as downtrodden sorrow.

A twinkling sense of humour shines through many of the fading pages, although mice and time have nibbled away a few chapters from this precious exercise book of memories.

It is too late to launch The Secret Diary of Hadrian Mule, aged 783/4 on the Christmas literary market, and so publication plans are being held back until the spring.

In the meantime, I am privileged to present a few short extracts from what is bound to be a bestseller for many years to come.

They show we had creative writers of quality long before the University of East Anglia was built. Hadrian's campus was the hedgerow and meadow, his classroom the local ale-house. He graduated with unsung honours to the candle-lit parlour where he studied and wrote, perhaps with no thought of posterity.

Praise and thanks may be long overdue, and social historians are just as excited as book people at the discovery. No living relatives have been traced yet, although certain names and locations are easily recognised despite the rough-and-ready spelling and erratic geography.

Hadrian employs words and expressions heard all too rarely these days, like "axed" for asked, "wittery" for weak, "soler" for a big one and "gays" for pictures in a book or magazine.

He "jam bowt" when he goes walking, and is "all of a dudder" when those lazy old winds go straight through him. He moans about "drafty old weather" when it's damp, raw and misty, and refers to any clumsy sort of fellow as a "great lummox".

He talks of a farming world dominated by men and horsepower, and a parish community where demarcation lines between the rulers and the ruled are clearly drawn.

Despite a growing awareness of union power among agricultural workers, and some radical sermons from the chapel pulpits, Hadrian's Norfolk still rests squarely on the "way things have allus been".

I risk incurring the wrath of Norfolk scholars, and devotees of the vernacular, in "transplanting" Hadrian's work into more orthodox language. Yes, it loses some of its flavour and much of its rhythm in being modernised, but I am anxious to present it to as wide an audience as possible at this stage, with the hope an "old-fashioned" power will return to pulsate through the full publication process.

The approach to Christmas early this century was a sedate affair compared with today's helter-skelter of commercialism. But it still provided social highlights and excuses for mild indulgence, as this extract from an early December entry illustrates: "Soon be time for Squire's Orange Round, and we hope Widow Long remembers to curtsey this year. Squire did not let his anger out over her ungracious ways, but she had to charm his warts away for no reward. Puckaterry Lister did not tug his forelock, but he has not done so these 20 years since he became bald as an egg.

"Always a good night at Inkaman (sic) Arms, and Squire's father and grandfather held event in high esteem as they bought down the family silver beet-hook for ceremonial slicing of the villagers' seasonal vitamins. All families take a segment with renewal of oath of allegiance, though cottagers down Podds Loke still talk of 1877 and how they were denied Yuletide treat because last orange that year was mildewed."

After all that juicy excitement down the local, home celebrations were bound to assume more modest levels. There was no great blow-out stretching over two or three days – just a simple but wholesome meal ready for noon on Christmas Day:

"Neighbour Jeremiah will join us this time now he is partly over death of Martha from the ague. No Norfolk man should be alone to take his onion gruel, fowl, oatcakes and plum pudding , and we can walk together up to the big house to receive our frumenty from squire's lady.

"Jeremiah will bring spiced elderberry wine left over from the funeral, but we cannot insist he wears a jolly hat or smile or plays our parlour games like Kiss in the Ring. While no man should be alone at this time, he is entitled to his own thoughts and a quiet corner."

Such a tolerant spirit would help keep many a gathering on the straight and narrow during the forthcoming season of peace, goodwill and over-heated expectations.

Hadrian's wall oven and ever-welcoming fire are the main planks for seasonable cheer, and he notes with enthusiasm the placing of the Yule Log, the largest block of elm he can find... "as long as it burns, my best cider will be served".

Apart from the tasty largesse handed out by a benevolent squirearchy, Hadrian and his rural contemporaries benefited from old-established local charities formed specifically to distribute a few extras at this time of the year.

Our newly-discovered correspondent sings the praises of the Browning brothers, Amos and Andrew, who set up a trust out of their estate to provide gravy for every Christmas meal within a six-mile radius of the thatched cottage where they lived all their lives.

"Oh, blessed are the homesteads where dumplings rise and wait for rich embellishment! The gravy mule-train is both a welcome sight and sound as we wait by the crackling hearth.

"Fill the basin and cover it with muslin, and then make more certain your name is on the list for next year. Have not missed the gravy train in two decades, and I pray to soak up my bread till my royal suit wears thin."

This sartorial reference evidently concerns Hadrian's excursions to Norwich in November, 1909, to catch a glimpse of Edward VII on his visit to the city. Indeed, our Norfolk diarist was well-travelled for his time, considering his humble status, and the final extract from this seasonal selection finds him relishing the prospect of another big outing: "Our procession will embark from the chapel steps at 6pm and there is brave talk of singing and collecting in two more parishes nearby this year. But I cannot see lantern, legs or voices holding out that long, especially if the weather is inclement.

" 'It Came Upon a Midnight Clear' remains my favourite for solo rendition, and is bound to be the subject of most requests. I will not be averse to rehearsal at Inkaman Arms some hours before it again rings across the farmyard with melodeon accompaniment."

***

DOUBLE TROUBLE
The newly-married Norfolk farm worker went to a lot of trouble over the white-washing of his cottage. Asked about his thoroughness, he replied: "The larst tew families what lived here hed twins. I'm just mearkin' sure there ent no infection!"

PULPIT PEELING

A Norfolk rector had as his churchwarden a chap called Ebenezer, who also had the job of looking after the rector's horses.

One day the rector came across Ebenezer standing idle in a field beside the plough and team, and asked why he wasn't working. Ebenezer said he was resting the horses.

"Well, my good man," said the rector, "next time you come out bring your hook, and while you are resting the horses, you can be busy trimming the hedge."

The following Sunday, when Ebenezer was on duty in church, the rector was most surprised to find on mounting the pulpit that it contained a knife and a bowl of potatoes.

After the service he asked his churchwarden why he had placed these curious objects there.

"Dew I kin trim a hidge tyme I'm a'restin' o' my hosses," said Ebenezer, "I rekun yew kin peel them spuds tyme yew're a'preachin' yar sarmun."

***

USEFUL LOSS
An agricultural worker went to a farmer for a job. He was asked for a character reference from his last employer.
"Well, marster, I did he'one, but I lorst it."
"Yew must be a fewl, a'losin' onnit like that" said the farmer.
"Nut such a fewl as yew think" said the worker. "Yew see, ol' bewty, I'd read it!"

BORING MUD CAN STICK

I used to think it was all the work of the local anti-tourist board – faceless fools with the temerity to question the power and benefits of the greatest growth industry in the world.

We had Norfolk branded the most unfriendly county in the United Kingdom, albeit an honour we had to share with Yorkshire, and Mileham singled out as the worst village in the country for accepting newcomers. (I was allowed in a few months ago because I happened to be born nearby.)

There were plenty more snipings before Fakenham got lumbered with an Oscar as Most Boring Place in the World. It was this award that convinced me more sinister forces could be in action.

There's been a lot of development round the edges of Fakenham in recent years – an idea they picked up from North Walsham, Wymondham, Dereham, Attleborough, Aylsham, Diss, Swaffham, Mulbarton, Hethersett and several others – and there was speculation more could be on the way.

Now, if there's not much to do in Fakenham, by day or by night, sensible people will shy away from moving into the area. They will head for the bright lights and fleshpots of more go-ahead places. Never mind all this twaddle about catering for youngsters, especially those on holiday; it is well-heeled, fun-loving folk on the doorstep who drive the local community.

With this in mind, it is a fair bet our old friends in the construction industry were behind this Fakenham character assassination. They want to pitch their tents and set their concrete mixers in motion in locations with a bit more space to spare and a few more attractions to entice.

My advice is clear. Beware a rash of planning applications for strip clubs at Wells, drinking dens at Docking, all-night casinos at Winfarthing, topless launderettes at Stoke Ferry, a drive-in cinema multiplex at Threxton and Irish theme pubs at Oby.

Rumours are circulating of similar forces at work in Suffolk, not least with the Skateboarding for the Over-80s campaign at Southwold and Bring Back the Charleston tea dances at Bungay.

This is an issue on which cross-border talks would prove useful. In the meantime, poor old Fakenham might well miss out on the joys of more development if some of this "boring" mud starts to stick.

PAST – OR FUTURE?

They came to resurface our road the other day. Men in brightly-coloured jackets formed an advance party, lorries and rollers thundering behind.

Before they could unleash their mixture of tar and chippings the street had to be cleared of all vehicles. An eerie silence fell on our little bit of Cromer as cars were spirited away, ours among them.

I strolled to the end of the road – a wide, empty road I had never seen before. Birdsong and the heavy scent of wall-flowers and lilac took over.

Several neighbours popped out to share an unlikely experience.

"We ought to hold a street party to celebrate!" quipped one. "Perhaps a horse and cart will come along in a minute to complete the old-fashioned picture," said another.

It didn't last long. The men, lorries and rollers left and the cars resurfaced to claim familiar berths against the pavement.

A silly, sentimental interlude left me baffled. Had I been peering into the past – or the future?

***

PUB SUB SNUB
Good yarn from Geoff Mallett of Clenchwarton following a mardle with colleagues about Norfolk people and Norfolk ways.
A lad left school and went to work on the fishing boats at Lynn for Jack Castleton. He had to work a week before getting paid, and on the Friday night discovered he had no money to join the others down the pub. He decided to ask the boss to help out:
Boy: Any chance of a sub till next week?
Jack: No, you'll have a fishing boat like the rest of 'em!

KING-SIZED AMBITIONS CAN COME TRUE

I fulfilled a long-standing fantasy the other evening. Well, as near as I am likely to get before this soccer season goes to ground.

Nudge Liverpool and Everton aside. Make way for Runton United and Sheringham in the Cromer Lifeboat Cup Final. For Wembley read Cabbell Park.

I was invited to present the trophy and medals to the winners, and to come up with a man of the match, a duty loaded with as many dangers as judging the fancy-dress contest at the village garden fete.

Runton won 3-2 against the cup holders, and Runton's composed No 6 Montague, was my choice as the final's top performer. The decision seemed a popular one.

However, the outstanding feature of the occasion was to shake hands with players and officials before the kick-off in true national stadium fashion.

You see, I have nursed this regal complex for a long time, ever since it became obvious Stanley Matthews and Tom Finney could get by without my wizardry on the pitch.

Cricketing aspirations took a similar turn after I had shared a few useful stands with Len Hutton, Denis Compton and Bill Edrich. I became satisfied with just being John Arlott, voice of summer, king of commentators, as I rode my bike and pretended to be singing if any heads should peer over passing hemlock.

Staying true to the premise that if you can't join 'em, you might as well talk or write about 'em, I embarked on a sports reporting career that began on raw afternoons at the likes of Cabbell Park over 25 years ago.

Three visits to Wembley with Norwich City convinced me I should have emerged from more noble stock. The urge to take a stately stroll down the red carpet with all the other dignitaries for knowing nods and firm handshakes became almost unbearable.

Indeed, the happiest of those final chapters, the Canaries' Milk Cup meeting with Sunderland in 1985, proved too much. I was King George V for part of the day.

I tell this story against myself mainly because I was seen masquerading in royal colours, and it remains important to prevent too many embellishments on the part of less-theatrical colleagues.

Wembley was all but deserted as we arrived to prepare for broadcasting duties, and it appeared safe to risk a quick wave from the Royal Box. Soon after, in the bowels of the stadium where stairs, stanchions, corners and cubby holes proliferate, I spied a giant mirror outside a gents' cloakroom. Too good a chance to let by.

Straightening shoulders, stroking beard and clearing throat, I moved serenely along the human tunnel. I wished the City players best of luck, accepting their bows with a benevolent smile. I knew all their names.

"All the best, Watson. Keep that green and yellow flying..."

"Good luck, Channon. Your experience will prove invaluable..."

"Ah, the manager. Greetings, Mr Brown. Let me just say..."

In fact, I dried up sharply. My two colleagues had collapsed in uncontrollable mirth in the doorway. Not at my virtuoso performance. They jabbed telling fingers towards a small shadowy corner of that capital stage. Leaning out of a small window was a small man with a big look of amazement on his face.

He had witnessed my regal cabaret with growing interest, while my two so-called friends had watched us both before their ribs started aching and the laughter had to come out.

I felt silly. And I felt sorry for the Sunderland players and match officials still waiting for a handshake and a word of encouragement.

"It's all right... he's from Norfolk, and you know what they're like when they get to London." The little attendant blinked at the explanation, nearly smiled and popped back into his little world of sanity and silence.

So, king-sized ambitions had been cut short, but I knew deep down another stage would present itself before life's final whistle. Cabbell Park at Cromer provided rich consolation, and my warmest thanks to Runton and Sheringham for playing their parts, albeit unwillingly, in my fantasy game.

***

LIGHT TOUCH
A Norfolk vicar vetoed a request by the parochial church council for a chandelier in church. He explained: "I would have to write the order for it and I can't spell the word. Furthermore, we have no one in the parish who can play it."

YEAR GROWS RIPE WITH THAT OLD ROMANCE

Despite my traumatic career as a helper in the local harvest fields just after the horses had gone, romantic images keep tugging me back while the wheat turns yellow and the year grows ripe.

They can't all be illusions carved out of a need to forget how those mechanical monsters of my teenage days left mental scars the size of freshly-plaited ricks.

The Fordson Major clutch was my biggest enemy, waiting to spring nasty little surprises as men perched perilously on top of the trailer loaded behind.

Some balancing acts would not have disgraced the Moscow State Circus. The language was undiluted Norfolk, leaving no doubt as to the pleasure my disappearance from the agricultural arena would afford those time-tanned sons of the stubble.

Before I heeded their advice and left the building of grain mountains to those of a more stable disposition, my tractor troubles culminated in the notorious stack-wrecking incident up Red Barn Hill.

To cut a tragic tale short, my Stirling Moss impression was wasted on Beeston brethren carefully constructing another straw temple to the harvest gods.

Confusion arose between clutch and brake. Allied to excessive speed, this meant a simple misjudgement en route to the elevator. One corner of the stack was trimmed out. I missed the other three. I ate my fourses alone.

It is a wonder I retain any affection at all for harvest time after such cruel treatment. Banishment on that hot August afternoon left me on the verge of complete retirement from farming chores. It was only when I heard distant colleagues planning a farewell collection that I decided to give them a few more days of unpredictable assistance.

Now, much older, much wiser, I take celebrated company with me whenever I step on to the harvest scene, still preferring to treat it as an archaic rite rather than a mechanical process.

Leading our little party bringing in the sheaves is a sadly-neglected woman from the golden days of vanished summers. Matilda Bertham-Edwards paraded "The Lord Of The Harvest" in 1899, a Suffolk idyll set in a rural community in the early years of Queen Victoria's reign.

Elisha Sage is the character with absolute authority for the duration of the reaping. This is the sort of stage over which he presided: "The sun sank behind the pollard oaks and twilight succeeded, hardly bringing coolness. A little later, although no breeze sprang up, pleasant freshness lightened their labours; another and yet another drink from the master's can lent new strength, long after moon rising, that mechanical swing of 20 arms, that gleam of 20 sickles went on.

"Deep almost solemn silence reigned over the cornfield. Only the rustle of footsteps and wheat falling on the stover broke the stillness, a stillness and monotony emblematic of these noiseless, unheroic lives, the tide of human existence that perpetually ebbs and flows, leaving no memory behind."

Comparing notes with Matilda is Henry Rider Haggard, Norfolk gentleman farmer, as well as famous author. On this day in 1898, he wrote in his diary, "A Farmer's Year", these harvest impressions: "The sight of the men, one following the other across the field in a jagged line as they cut down the ripe corn with wide sweeps of the scythe, makes a fine picture of effort strenuous and combined. The place is pretty too, with the windmill in the background, and the heat-haze softening the scene, keeping it in tone and making it restful.

"One of the features of these mowings is the almost inevitable presence of a man with a dog – someone in the village who is fond of a bit of sport. As the mowers approach the end of a stretch, a bunny or two will bolt, and be swept up by the dog before it can win the shelter of the hedge."

A mere half-century ago, Henry Williamson was the dreamer coming face to face with reality. He joins our band of cornfield workers with a telling extract from "The Story Of A Norfolk Farm", the account of his first two years as an amateur farmer: "I looked forward to the harvest, as a time of purification. It was exhausting work, but it drew the poison of immobility out of the system. It was sweaty work, lifting the sheaves on to the wagon, then from the wagon to the stack. We had no mechanical elevator...

"Anxiously we watched dark thunder clouds moving around us, now over the sea, now over the distant horizon. But we were lucky; no tempest fell upon us. Some farms a few miles away lost much of their corn, beaten down by terrific hailstorms, which killed half-grown lambs, shattered plants of sugar-beet and mangold, and stripped hundreds of acres of standing barley."

That poet among modern ecologists, John Stewart Collis, also worked on the land in the 1940s. He opens his rucksack to share "The Worm Forgives The Plough". The power of the combine harvester goes against the grain: "The age-long, centuries-old tradition of harvesting, of gathering up the year's work, is taken away from the labourers. In their place the one big machine, We look across the land for human beings, and we see – one engine. And in its wake the bare field; no ricks meet the eye and no work for thatchers or threshers."

Other sensitive souls wait on the headlands to join our scything away the summers. There's Adrian Bell, townsman turned farmer, who wrote with such beauty of both men and the fields, and C. Henry Warren, whose "Corn Country" reminds us that "every tractor driver, doing his three acres a day with the plough, is direct heir to the Neolithic tribesman scratching the meagre surface of his upland patch with a red deer's antler."

There's A. G. Street, no stranger to Norfolk meadows, drawing comparisons with his native Wiltshire, and reminding us how dear old Richard Jeffries had claimed in 1879 that the next generation of country folk would hardly be able to understand the story of Ruth.

Mr Street brings echoes from 1935: "The combine harvester has robbed the harvest field of as much charm for me as the self-binder did for Jeffries. He mourned the passing of the gleaners, and I feel tempted to mourn the passing of the sheaf and the stook. It is the same old story – each new method, while it may increase the efficiency of farming, robs my calling of some of its romance and charm."

The sun goes down, albeit reluctantly. Robert Bloomfield, "The Farmer's Boy" of 1800, is heard but not seen with just two of the lines he composed in a London garret:

Calm dreams of bliss bring
on the morning sun,
For every barn is fill'd
and Harvest done!

***

THEY DEW SAY
Horry: Woss the diffrunce atwin remember an' recerllect?
Tom: Wuh, there ent no diffrunce.
Horry: Dew yew remember that five quid I lent yer?
Tom: Yeh...
Horry: Well, I dunt recerllect gettin' the beggar back!

DALE TO RESCUE

My Mundesley adventure began with the purchase of a straw hat to replace a tattered object letting in the rain after several summers of service.

I sauntered along the seafront catwalk, waved to the man looking out from the Maritime Museum and took a seat to savour my whirly ice-cream.

A puckish gust lifted my smart hat from its new home. It flew over the railings and landed half-way down the steep slope to the beach. My wife voted against a solo rescue mission. I didn't fancy going either.

The man looking out from the Maritime Museum opened his window and said he did not have a pole long enough to aid any recovery plans. I asked the wife to keep an eye on the errant headgear while I sent for reinforcements.

When I reached the beach and revealed my sad little plight to the lifeguards they were ready for action. Dale, bronzed and enthusiastic, led the charge uphill and downhill as if he were on castors.

He handed over the hat with an "all part of the job" nod and smile. I promised to keep it out of the draughts.

The man looking out from the Maritime Museum must have thought it all rather exciting for a Monday.

We settled for a quiet spell inland after that, picking strawberries at Antingham

"Punnet" said the wife. So I did. "Bound to end in the second jam of the day." I pulled down the hat to cover my shame.

***

PLAYING WITH FIRE
A tramp on his way from Ipswich to Norwich came to the George and Dragon Inn. He decided to try his luck.
His knock on the back door summoned the landlady who shouted: "Clear off, you lazy good-for-nothing creature!" She slammed the door in his face.
As he turned towards the open road again, the tramp passed the open kitchen window.
He pushed his head through and asked: "Any chance of a word with George?"

A BELATED PLEA FOR BRECKLAND'S SOUL

It was hardly love at first sight. To be frank, there was little to suggest our relationship would stretch beyond the few months we were fated to share.

My first thoughts in deepest Breckland, on a glowing-red Sunday evening in September, 1962, were fixed on those uniform regiments of trees playing hide-and-seek with the setting sun. The monotony reinforced my sadness on leaving home.

Uncle Cyril did his best to cheer me up as his van coughed politely past the forest sentries, tall, silent sentries watching an apprehensive lad from the middle of Norfolk following a trail carved out by thousands of Londoners.

I was destined for Thetford and my first job as a junior reporter on the local newspaper. (Picture the scene, hum the music and we'll call this "All Features Great and Small"). I knew a bit about Tom Paine and his Rights of Man, William George Clarke, who gave the region its name in 1894, and Grimes Graves. I had heard about overspill.

This was the place to see stuffy old Norfolk changing gear and driving down a different track. New factories, new estates and new horizons in one of Britain's fastest-growing towns. I couldn't make any instant comparisons, but I soon began to wish I had come when it was all rather homely and unexciting.

Simple instincts told me chopping off a chunk of capital sprawl and trying to attach it to a modest country town would not rank as the most progressive example of social surgery this century.

Such sentiments seem to be finding countless echoes in today's protests against the imposition of unnatural growth on the county as a whole. But it is not my purpose here to pursue all-too-familiar arguments. I just want to make a plea for Breckland's soul.

I realise now it was bidding for my attention over a quarter-of-a-century ago when I had occasion to escape from town into forest and heath. Derelict villages, deserted churches and ancient tracks cried out for longer inspections, but the atmosphere was too strong, too strange for an apprentice inspector.

Perhaps the ghosts of Breckland past were themselves unnerved by the obvious presence of military machinations. An uneasy co-existence at best between troops and locals who could not forget how the Battle Area was born out of war and the evacuation of five villages – Stanford, Lynford, Tottington, West Tofts and Buckenham Tofts. A moment's silence for those who fell...

Yes, I did make tentative inquiries about the real Breckland at a time when so much was changing beyond the tall, silent sentries. I marked Santon Downham, pretty, cosy Santon Downham, as a possible retirement location in an unlikely burst of long-term planning.

But I never dared get close enough to worry about Breckland's soul – a soul that inspired historian and naturalist William George Clarke to shave with a prehistoric flint implement he found near Brandon.

Strangely, my concern has grown since I started to keep a daily diary in the past few years. Virtually every reference to Breckland has involved a commercial or military threat to what remains of the primeval spirit. The area, it seems, is ripe for a new kind of exploitation, with the burgeoning tourist trade poised to make the biggest killing. The holiday village at Elveden, due to open shortly with a mighty fanfare, could well be a tree-lined trailblazer.

Plans for more holiday and leisure facilities are bound to multiply, despite recent failures to win permission to go ahead on various sites, including the edge of the Euston Estate and in homespun Santon Downham.

You will recall how East Wretham villagers fought long and hard against the scheme to build an Army battle training village near their homes. Questions about "Army Games" reached The Commons, the story was on the BBC national news, where they called the settlement "Reefham", and the Army pledged their "helicopters will be quiet ones."

There have been several protest movements in the small Breckland communities against schemes to extend the training area, and the army dropped plans to buy the Hilborough Estate just when it seemed they were on the verge of widening their empire.

There are persistent rumours that acres of forest could become a nuclear dumping ground. Members of the "No To Nirex" group refuse to be placated by statements about no firm decision being made yet.

Growing pressures from several sides, fuelled, one suspects, by the feeling there's so much room in wild and woolly Breckland, certain plans are bound to get the nod if you are persistent enough.

I recall how, in May, 1987, the area came in for sharp criticism for not doing enough to push the tourism bandwagon. A Worcester firm was commissioned by Breckland council to present a tourism strategy.

Their report said the council could approach the Forestry Commission over the change of status of Thetford Forest to a forest park to enable greater funding for recreation and tourism. It was also suggested that the battle area ought to be turned into a tourist attraction. Breaks for relatives of American servicemen stationed at nearby bases was another idea.

John Birkbeck (who else!) urged caution in making provision for tourists with this memorable response: "Show me a place that has been improved by tourists, and I will show you a hundred that have been wrecked by them."

That report surfaced just 11 days after Breckland was officially recognised for its great conservation value, and designated an Environmentally Sensitive Area, stretching from near Bury St Edmunds, up towards Lakenheath, Feltwell, Methwold and across to Swaffham, down towards South Pickenham, Watton, East Harling and Garboldisham.

Farmers and landowners would qualify for substantial cash incentives to protect old meadows, grassland and other areas of wildlife value. What price an Environmentally Sensitive Area against the speculators and spoilers armed with market forces and a piece of paper from Worcester?

It may be too simple to call it a struggle between caravans and stone curlews. But there are confusions over priorities among those who make the big decisions, and those confusions must lead to collisions. A new battle area in Breckland.

Edward Storey, a writer doing for the Fens today what Michael Home did for Breckland with his novels half-a-century ago, says: "There is a certain spirit about a place which makes it different from all other places." I know now what he means when I salute the tall, silent sentries.

There are relics of prehistory everywhere in Breckland. It has more links with the faraway past than almost any other part of the country. Airfields, military exercises, factories, estates, busy main roads, caravan sites... all have been defied to a considerable extent. Now the interlopers are bigger and brasher.

A belief in Breckland fairies persisted for a long time, inspired by the small, dark Neolithic people who came from Spain, Portugal and Brittany. Invaders of the final part of the 20th century are likely to arouse more suspicion that superstition. If those suspicions are confirmed, Breckland's soul will be borne away on a cruel, unforgiving wind.

CHUCKLES WITH CHARLIE

A drop of homespun humour can enliven the most mundane of occasions, a point well underlined in a letter from Philip Harpley of Acle. He was called up to join the 7th Battalion of the Royal Norfolk Regiment at Woolaton Park just outside Nottingham in 1940. One of his colleagues was Charlie Buck, a farm worker from Scottow and "a real Norfolk character".

Philip recalled the first pay parade when they lined up in alphabetical order as the sergeant major told them what to do – march up to the tables, salute the officers, hand over the paybook and then move to the colour sergeant to sign for the pay, the princely sum of five shillings.

Charlie was one of the first. When he reached the colour sergeant he collected a sharp rebuke: "Look at your hands, Buck. They're filthy. How dare you come on pay parade with hands like that!"

Charlie replied in a broad Norfolk accent: "I're bin a'lookin at yars, Govner, an' they ent nun tew bludder bright!"

There was quite an uproar, and even the officers burst out laughing.

CHALKY CATERPILLARS

Looks like another bumper crop of roadside apostrophes coming up this season. Some of the abbreviations are bad enough – it was years before someone told me PYO doesn't stand for Paston Youth Orchestra – but the tiny chalky caterpillars crawling all over the fruit and vegetables simply reinforce my view that growers and sellers have forgotten the three Rs – Rhubarb, Radish and Red beet.

Perhaps those caterpillars will disappear if we ignore all the turnip's, cabb's, cauli's, rasp's, straw's, tom's, pot's and lett's. Nor should we encourage crab's and shrimp's, choc ice's and afternoon tea's... or even coach partie's. Let's put a full stop to the unwanted apostrophe.

THAT'S SALLE

I am receiving regular reports of strange noises and funny looks in the Reepham area. Music-loving folk heading for concerts in the village church are taxing local pride and patience with their requests for directions. They are tripping over one of Norfolk's most celebrated molehills – and making mountains of mistakes over Salle. Some natives refuse to recognise anything other than the proper pronunciation. So in the interests of peace co-existence and Norfolk culture, let me emphasise yet again that Salle is pronounced Saul.

This little tongue-twister might help:

Soulful Sally Saul whose sisters stay at Sporle and Stanninghall set out her stall in the aisle for a sale of work at St Peter and St Paul, Salle.

PROPER HOPES

Delightful evidence from Phil Bradstreet of Morley St Botolph that "proper Norfolk" is far from dead and buried.

Phil was at the Norfolk Show watching cattle come up the walkway and into the ring. Nearby were two smartly-dressed "town gals who could hardly tell a bull from a china shop".

A cow and calf appeared on the scene and suddenly stopped. "Whatever is that calf doing?" asked one of the ladies.

A little Norfolk lad about four years old, "his fearce like the moon a'cummin' up over the muck-heap", provided the answer.

"Thass arter a tit!" he explained. The ladies were grateful for enlightenment.

Phil celebrated: "If there are still people out there who teach little boys to talk properly, Norfolk will be here for a long time to come."

THE GENUINE ARTICLE

When I first became hooked on the delights of Norfolk dialect writing, I thought Ida Fenn was a made-up name. It sounded too good to be true!

But the woman who wove so many colourful yarns out of her rural experiences had no need of a non de plume. She had served her Norfolk apprenticeship by the time she married farmworker Harry Fenn.

Ida was born in London in 1899. Her father died when she was a baby and she moved to Weston Longville, a few miles from Norwich, to be brought up by her grandparents at Top Farm. Grandfather Walston Goward, mentioned in many of her stories, worked with horses at Weston Hall.

After working as a decorator and teaching at the village school, Ida married and during the 1930s her husband was a farm steward at St Faiths. With the outbreak of war the land was requisitioned to become an aerodrome (later Norwich Airport).

Ida and Harry lived on farms at Costessey and Winterton before buying Lyngate Farm, at Hethersett.

They were completing the deal when Harry died in 1955. Ida decided to carry on running the farm herself, and it was from this experience that she was able to write a weekly farming column as well as continuing with her popular Tales of a Countryman.

Her most regular contributions were to the Yarmouth Mercury where for over 20 years she supplied tales of the Boy Jimma and his family.

Ida wrote many other articles for magazines and two novels set in Norfolk, but it is for her tales of the countryman that she is most fondly remembered.

I turn to them when I feel in need of a testing dialect refresher course, for Ida wrote in the broad Norfolk of the Fleggs. Much of her writing was done while she farmed at Winterton, and a collection of her best village stories was first published in 1973.

Eric Fowler – Jonathan Mardle of the EDP – praised them as the genuine article: "If some people find the spelling hard to follow, let them be patient with it; for this language, as Mrs Fenn writes it, is about as near to the peculiar sound of broad Norfolk as you can get by setting it down on paper."

Try this for starters, the opening paragraph of the first chapter of Tales of a Countryman. It helps if you read it out loud:

"Our parish be like a lot more, there be plenty new housen

gorn up ivv'ry deer, but ours, they're like they wore when Faar wooz faast marrit an cam' ter live there. Thart wooz afore I wooz thowt on, well, leastways thass what he tell me."

It carries a rustic lyricism all its own, befitting of a special area lying between the sea and the Broads and, until comparatively recent years, often regarded as a separate province cut off from the rest of Norfolk.

Ida Fenn died in 1980, her place secure in any list of outstanding contributors to Norfolk dialect literature. She waved the flag for the old Fleggs with relish.

THE DAY WE MET NULL AND VOID

It was standing room only as we said farewell to Les Gould at Gorleston Crematorium.

Bunched at the back with several former newspaper colleagues, I tried to brush aside a jocular thought. It refused to go away.

Surely Les would have managed to include everyone present on the same picture for this final edition, and to make sure the multitude was captioned properly, left to right, top to bottom, seated and standing.

Still perched precariously on a makeshift podium, he would have employed his catchphrase "just one more" as insurance against any possible gremlins in the darkroom.

A man of many endearing idiosyncrasies, photographer Les inspired more yarns and smiles than is customary at a funeral. It was the right occasion for a dash or two of self-indulgence.

Tributes to his work for local newspapers from the Yarmouth base he found in 1949 have been paid in full by those who plied their trade alongside him over many years. As a young reporter at the resort in the mid-Sixties, I got to know him better than most... when he became my benevolent landlord.

There has been many a theory about the bottom of Les Gould's garden and my arrival as a lodger at the height of the holiday season. I believe the shed had been acquired as potential photographic unit for elder son Ivan, but it was really waiting for a waif-like figure with nowhere to rest his little head.

A shortage of funds, brought about largely by extra-mural activities in the name of investigative journalism around local hostelries, left me without regular digs. The prospect of a few thoughtful nights under the Britannia Pier carried limited appeal.

Les, ahead of his time when it came to potential causes of pollution, said I would be much safer, and so would the North Sea, if the offer of temporary quarters at the foot of his Gorleston garden was accepted.

A truly blissful phase of my life followed, although I had to put up with reveille on a hunting-horn from newspaper colleague Mike Farman, domiciled on the other side of the street in a reformed railway carriage called "Mutinette."

Certain other escapades with the ebullient Farman are being saved for a chapter of my autobiography, "One Pressman is worth Twenty Volunteers", but we did find complete harmony on that glorious afternoon when we watched England's 1966 World Cup triumph on the Gould family television set.

By now I had been invited indoors as a paying guest of the respectable kind, landlady Dorothy clearly impressed by my apprenticeship down the garden path. I was cared for regally during the rest of my reporting stint on the Mercury, sharing a host of assignments with the diligent Les and working overtime to find new excuses for being a few hours late for our evening meal.

Now and again, it was our own fault. Someone would mention the spoons at a flagging function and Les did not like to disappoint those who admired his impromptu musical talents.

Now and again, Les would get drawn into a bout of yarn-telling. He didn't so much go round the houses as move to another estate. He had a delicious habit of interrupting himself and then correcting himself, an art often mimicked by colleagues but never with a grain of malice.

"Now let me see. Must have been George Formby at the Windmill in... no, hang on. I tell a lie, It was Jimmy Clitheroe at the Brit. Yes, definitely him, and I ought to remember because that was the summer he asked to borrow my steps so he could reach his coat on the top peg in the Mayor's Parlour at that reception when the dancing girls..."

Now and again, Les would lose his thread altogether, and suggest it was my turn to take the flak if we happened to get home before sunrise.

He found it hard to relax away from his work, although he was persuaded to take a break in Southern Ireland in 1966. I joined him, Dorothy and younger son John on my first trip to the Emerald Isle.

Les betrayed early withdrawal symptoms as he scanned Dublin for a copy of the EDP. A tour round the offices of The Cork Examiner helped him settle. A drop of draught Guinness lured out the spoons in a couple of bars where culture was encouraged.

With a premonition perhaps, that I might be glad of a ready tongue in pursuit of employment on the wireless in later years, Les urged me to kiss the Blarney Stone. He recorded the touching scene for posterity as I turned 40 shades of green.

Comic highlight of the holiday bubbled up in a wayside cafe off the tourist track when two ancient women, all wrinkles and shawls, mustered something with beans out of a cauldron in the tiny back room. When they declined to have their likenesses taken, clearly believing we were spies for the Egon O'Ronay Good Food Guide, Les simply could not credit anyone could shy away from his camera.

"Good job Null and Void didn't see me taking a picture of them licking the spoon before they brought the plates in!"

Just one more: possibly the best illustration of the distinctive Les Gould character came during my early days as a colleague on the local paper. He had complained to Wilfred Bunting, the Mercury editor, and to Joe Harrison, the EDP chief reporter upstairs, about the number of jobs he'd been asked to do on his days-off. Of course, he did them all.

And that was Les. Never enough time, but enough energy and dedication to get round that. He came from the old school of newspapermen. I am proud to have been his pupil and his friend.

***

TROUBLE SHARED
I dropped in as usual at Cromer Junior School on a Wednesday morning to listen to some of the children reading.
An eight-year-old girl with a soft voice and a winning smile was caught out by the word "disintegrate". I tried to help by splitting it up – "dis-int-e-grate".
She looked up from her book and said quietly: "Oh, you have trouble with that one as well, do you?"

TRUE FACTS ABOUT OUR FEATHERED FRIEND

If confession is good for the soul, I am ready for Judgement Day. Well, all right... slightly better prepared than last month.

Dark episodes from my past have been forced into the open by a chain of events surely linked by divine intervention.

It all began at Ingoldisthorpe with the voluntary-aided first school's 130th anniversary celebrations. An afternoon packed with pictures from yesterday, in the classroom and on the playing field.

A powerful voice said it was time to do penance as they called up runners for the Gentlemen's Egg and Spoon Race. I sensed I was on a hiding to nothing as frisky rivals champed at the bit in the paddock and mocked my bravado in suggesting it would take experience rather than fitness to claim an Olympic qualifying time.

My first outing in this event since Beeston's Coronation Stakes on Lew Dack's buttercup-soaked meadow in 1953. I cheated then, thumb firmly on the egg for all but the last few yards of the village charge for a shiny new sixpence.

They cheered. I smiled, and fell over deliberately in the sack race. That coin became a lead weight in my pocket for the rest of the summer. I just could not let go of the guilt.

For all I know, others may have employed equally steadying thumbs or even smuggled chewing-gum beneath the shell. But I won that race and it was not fair.

No qualms at Ingoldisthorpe. I played it by the book and finished next to last. It was a wonderful feeling, a tingling release from the shackles I placed upon myself 35 years before.

The next instalment of my conscience-salving serial unfolded on a train journey back to Cromer. A tall Australian, recently retired and doing The Grand Tour of Northampton, Norwich and the North Norfolk coast, showed me the sunglasses he'd never worn in this country. We chatted about sport.

He used to be a full-time table tennis coach, and Australia had climbed to 25th in the world rankings. Not bad, considering most of his countrymen play outside games, like wrestling crocodiles. We turned to cricket and some epic confrontations made for sharing when rain sheets down and a signalmen's dispute brings an unscheduled stop at North Walsham.

The golden summer of 1953 returned to demand another confession. I told my new-found friend how I should have been fruit-picking or bean-pulling when England won back The Ashes with a victory at The Oval.

Compton and Edrich were at the crease. I was round Rex Howe's house listening to the wireless commentary, waiting to celebrate with jam sandwiches and a bottle of cold tea. Jubilation gave way to the jitters as going-home time beckoned.

I compiled a list of "explanations" for possible use in the event of being asked to produce the day's wages towards a new blazer for next term. A puncture, bad headache, looked like rain, they were shut, forgot all about it, helped distressed farmer whose cows had got out, kidnapped by bandits just outside Gressenhall, had a religious experience at Longham....

There were no questions, no showdown, but sleep was most uneasy. Another little secret I hid for 35 years until a chatty Aussie came along.

Terrington St Clement WI members, with friends from neighbouring institutes, were privy to an admission regarding important events from an even earlier date. I was in full cry about childhood and the village school when I let slip the fact that one of my sisters went with me on my visits to the outside toilets. I needed assistance to get my jersey off.

A lady, creased in mirth, asked why I had to take my jersey off. Good question, my dear, but it was so long ago I can't remember. Another chortler, with highly practical sons of her own, came to the rescue. It was the way to a lad's braces, and there was no time for hold-ups when urgent duties called.

The latest baring of my soul concerns an episode that has been the subject of far too much loose gossip. Not so much a confession as a belated but sincere attempt to put the record straight about The Gassing of Mrs P's Budgie.

Mrs P was my landlady for over a decade. She invited me to her birthday party last weekend to show we are still good friends. As I passed on greetings over the wireless the following day, I was challenged yet again to deny I had attempted to cut off the little pet bird in his prime. These are the facts...

I was alone in the house except for a small menagerie of pets. I discovered the cooker for the first time in an undistinguished culinary career. Beans on toast, without burning either, represented a major breakthrough. In my triumph, I forgot to turn off the gas after blowing out the flame.

My error was pointed out in a distraught telephone call to the office about seven hours later. Mrs P's dogs, Pepe and Bruce, had water eyes and nasty tizzicks in the throat. Mrs P's cat, Timmy, had watery eyes and a pronounced cough. Mrs P's budgie, Colin, had keeled over.

Mrs P, providentially, had not lit up her customary cigarette on arriving home. She no longer smokes, and I like to think I played a small part in helping her kick the habit.

I was so upset by the whole business, I took refuge in a colleague's home for the night. I was requested to keep out of the kitchen and urged to make my peace with old friends the following morning. As long as they were still capable of offering an audience.

Colin took longest to recover. I carried daily bulletins to work where comments like "you ought to be up before the beak" did little to ease my conscience.

Mrs P, renowned for her charitable instincts, has exonerated me from all malicious intent, despite once catching me in an attempt to silence our feathered friend with the Rothman's Football Year Book from a considerable distance. She understood my frustration at missing half the soccer results through garrulous interruptions.

So, let there now be an end to scurrilous stories about bids to sent Colin to that Great Cagebird Society In The Sky long before his millet ran out or his mirror and ladder were reclaimed by the budgie bailiffs.

We may not have been bosom pals, but we respected each other's rights in Mrs P's kingdom. And he did me one good turn.

I never had to cook my own breakfast again. Now, who's a clever boy, then!

***

CORNY REPLY
A Norfolk farmer said to one of his workers: "Blarst, yew're gettin' wholly bent in the back. I'm older than yew but I'm still as streart as a gun barrel!"
The old worker simply pointed to a field of corn.
"Woss that get t'dew with it?" asked the farmer.
The worker smiled...
"Well, yew see all them wi' full hids are bent over. All th'empty ones are streart up."

LET'S MEET FARMER ON HIS OWN MIDDEN

One of my favourite yarns features some young lads from London who were evacuees on a Norfolk farm during the war.

The farmer had promised to take them to market in his horse and cart. They waited excitedly by this new form of transport, when one little boy ran into the house yelling: "Come quick, mister, the horse is losing all its petrol!"

There are countless other stories designed to underline the ignorance of town and city dwellers when it comes to life down on the farm. Laughter is laced with pity rather than malice.

But just how honest is that laughter these days? How many people living in Norfolk, still a predominantly agricultural county, would pass a simple test in farming matters?

Let's narrow it down even more. How many inhabitants of any six Norfolk villages taken at random would be able to chat easily about agricultural topics with the local farmer?

Precious few, I suggest, could argue coherently for or against the set-aside scheme, milk quotas or nitrate levels. Does it really matter? Depends on how you see the role of the farmer in the continuing saga of fast-changing Norfolk.

I maintain his part is one of the most significant as the cast assembles for the final act of the century. Farmers, love them or lambast them, featherbed them or cut off their subsidies, will spend a lot more time in the spotlight before we turn that big corner into the 21st century.

Solid enough a reason, then, to call for a new relationship between sons of the soil and the rest of us – especially those computerised cousins who feel they might have something in common after all with high-tech agribusiness.

Long gone are the days when the bulk of the population would need merely a glance over the hedge to identify the crop, to determine the state of that crop and to make instant comparisons with crops of the previous five years.

Virtually every family had close connections with the land, some of them sinking deep into Norfolk's past. Few of those roots remain in a world where the prairie and a lone ranger in a cab have taken over from the meadow and a posse of country thoroughbreds.

The farmer's status in the community has diminished

alongside traditional dependence on him for employment and shelter. Mechanisation has pulled down history's hedgerows, but there's no room to turn round for a gentle stroll down yesterday's furrows... unless you believe in marketing forces.

Advertising agencies, obviously overloaded with refugees from the Saturday morning mucking-out club, feed us country goodness, country freshness and Mummerzet magic till it comes over the top of our green wellies.

Cherish those lovely moments when the pod goes pop in the glistening dew; Rover jogs off to round up the cows and he'd probably milk 'em as well if you'd let him; the rosy-cheeked ploughman pats his waiting stomach as his rosy-cheeked wife brings in the first of six naturally healthy courses; ducks and hens scatter as Postman Pete smiles his way up the village street.

The countryside is packaged that way, and no-one has the heart to fall out with such cosy images until something like The Great Egg Scare comes along. Suddenly, food production is a subject for prolonged scrutiny on Panorama. Pressure groups go on the warpath. Hygiene experts go on television. British Food and Farming Year does not seem such a smart idea after all.

Farmers go red in the face, and not just for bucolic effect. They point to incomes at an all-time low and increasing public demands for cheap food produced by what they prefer to call "modern" rather than "intensive" methods. They accuse the consumer and the media of over-reacting, and launch a public relations exercise to put them straight.

Perhaps that gap between slick advertisers' romanticising and the agricultural reality is simply too wide for the sides to meet on a commonsense bridge. A fluffy chick and salmonella cannot possibly belong to the same world!

Now, we need much more than a public relations drive to carve out a worthwhile footpath into a rapidly-changing farming arena. The need to explain modern methods is more important than the urge to employ them just to keep up with demand.

I often sense farmers are too eager to condemn our criticisms as nothing more than proof positive of crass ignorance, without taking any steps to lighten our darkness.

We can be equally dismissive, treating them as some corduroyed freemasonry of the fields and flocks, constantly complaining about everything and being liberally subsidised by a benevolent Government for doing so.

If farmers do have plenty to answer for – and they cannot hide every mountain of moans behind Ministry instructions of the day

– they must be asked the right questions. Then, if they refuse to give direct responses, future complaints about "over-reacting" will be treated with disdain.

For our part, we must accept certain facts. Many farmers are locked into investment in the cause of providing our cheap food, although some are clearly unsettled by the pace of scientific change and increased risks involved.

They all know tastes and attitudes will continue to change – organic methods are winning fresh support every day – and that they will be asked to keep up with trends.

Even so, it is not just our stomachs that matter. What we see going on in the name of farming will continue to be mighty important, especially as the diversification bandwagon gathers speed.

Exemption of farming from many planning controls can result in eyesores on the landscape. Advice on conservation matters can be sought from the local farming and wildlife advisory group. But its entirely voluntary natures means many of those responsible for major changes in the rural landscape are the very ones most likely to shun the opportunities it offers.

Farmers like to be called "custodians of the countryside", but there are too many involved with proposed schemes for more big housing developments across the region to take that title very seriously.

Indeed, some are prepared to come out of the cartshed and queue up with the developers to offer multi-million pound packages to improve or provide local facilities in return for permission to build homes on land not scheduled for housing.

So, as pressures and inducements multiply, we must show our concern by trying to meet the farmer on his own midden. Of course, some stage open days, and several are forging strong links with local schools. But there is ample room for closer ties between an oft-suspicious public and an industry reluctant to go far beyond the hand-out from an NFU spokesman.

If British Rail can urge us to adopt a local station, The Norfolk Way Of Life Department has every right to suggest that idea be extended across the headlands and into the farmyard.

I reckon a better-informed neighbour and consumer could well help agriculture see its problems and challenges in a brighter light.

Find a farmer and have a meaningful mardle today. If you see one on a bike, be polite and wait till he parks.

GIVE YOURSELF A BIT OF STICK!

As the nights pull in quicker than a beer belly on the beach when a bikini-clad lass comes into view, so the annual dinner season calls for attention.

It is a lengthy season, fraught with danger for those called upon to inform the assembled company that it is indeed a pleasure and a privilege to be with them on this auspicious occasion.

In the first place, they might not believe you, however sincere you sound or look. Openly hostile or uncannily quiet, they can make you feel like Ken Livingstone dropping in on the Conservative Party Conference.

As a reporter on our local newspapers, I sat through hundreds of functions with their speeches of varying length and quality. The perfect apprenticeship for someone now being asked to sing for his supper on a regular basis.

I recall one amiable but fairly unimaginative dignitary on the local dinner circuit about two decades ago who had the same speech for all occasions. It was my good fortune to be pencilled in to hear him a dozen times in one calendar month. (Seven chicken main courses, four turkey and one roast beef.)

He simply changed the name of the club or organisation to fit the bill. I don't think many of them knew he was coughing up a replay with slight amendments.

I amused myself by miming his words as he jogged along, and noting reactions to limp yarns in a threadbare repertoire. (Seven titters, four yawns and one "when will he get to the punchline?")

How he beamed on sitting down to polite applause! Possibly out of a mixture of sheer relief and rejoicing at getting away with it yet again.

Still, I know now he was sent to test my journalistic qualities and powers of imagination, because I had to come up with a fresh flavour for each report without mentioning the menu.

One stroke that roving repeater did not pull was to try to involve the rest of the top table in the battle for attention. You know... outrageous gestures, desperate smiles from side to side, knowing nudges, all designed to earn a collective sympathy from other honoured guests in the hope of it spreading round the room.

Of course, many have speech-making thrust upon them by

office or position in the community. You can see some of them wondering if the chain or badge is really worth all this shredding of nerves.

It is hard to muster brevity or wit as you wipe a perspiring forehead with crumpled notes and then try to read your serviette.

While certain formalities ought to be observed, like getting the toast and responses in order and waiting for permission to smoke or go home, after-dinner sessions should be relatively relaxed and entertaining.

Here are a few handy tips I've collected over the years...

It is folly to start with your funniest story. An audience likes to be teased and built up, not sent crashing downhill among the coffee cups and cigar smoke.

Self-denigration can be most useful. After giving yourself a bit of stick, it is much more acceptable to get stuck into some of the miscreants who have seen fit to mock your idiosyncrasies.

A word of warning here. Check with wives, husbands or loved ones that your prospective targets do have a sense of humour. Familiarity has been known to breed contempt at the annual bunfight, even if it is hidden under a smirk.

Never be coarse for the sake of it, although it should be noted that certain Norfolk yarns warrant an earthy coating. And don't be scared of changing course in the middle of a speech when reaction, or lack of it, tells you this could be useful or even a means of salvation.

Do not smother your audience in gratuitous praise, even if they are celebrating a string of outstanding achievements. If your jokes fall flat, don't blame someone else for passing them on to you in the first place. That's just the same as a centre-forward cursing the ball or the pitch when he misses an open goal.

Remember, your audience are there for a big night on the social calendar. It could be the only function they attend all year and dinners are expensive.

Short speeches can be just as uplifting or embarrassing as long ones, although the only certainty in this social jungle is that guarantees don't come with the wine.

Last week's winner at West Winch can be tonight's clanger at Clenchwarton, while a little aside can spark the sort of mirth Eric Morecambe unleashed every time he waggled his glasses or picked up a plastic cup.

I once saw a council chairman about to disappear under the top table in a lather of indifference when a woman wandered into the banqueting hall by mistake. She responded willingly to his stumbling inquiries and they proceeded to bring the house down with delightful ad-libbing.

"Do you come here often?" – "Only when there's somebody good on" – "So, what brings you here this evening?" – "My old man, and I think I'll join him down the pub."

Visiting speakers, some of whom can command extravagant fees, get short measure if they are too patronising or take liberties with vernacular best left to the natives. Compulsive name-droppers, especially from the world of sport, have been known to provoke snorts of disapproval long before the first waltz.

I suppose much of it boils down to sheer instinct, although you should have done some homework out of the fundamental desire for self-preservation.

Perhaps the dilemma is best illustrated by the markedly different receptions afforded to the two after-dinner speakers using the same opening gambit at functions I attended a few years ago.

At the cricket dinner, this went down a treat: "This is the second time this evening I have risen from a warm seat with a piece of paper in my hand."

At a local firm's annual shindig, it struck stony ground. The speaker was left naked, apart from the fig leaf he made out of his official invitation.

***

BREATHLESS SPELL
The headmaster's study in a Norfolk school was up a flight of stairs. One morning there was a knock on the door. A stout woman entered, very much out of breath.
"Now, what can I do for you?" asked the headmaster.
His visitor puffed and panted. "I couldn't send my mawther Mary ter school terday."
"Well, why didn't you send me a note then?"
"But I couldn't let mawther Mary cum ter school terday."
"Yes, but surely a note would have sufficed."
"Blarst, yew dunt think I would ha' climbed all these bloomin' steps, dew yer," said the breathless one, "if I could ha' spelt diarrhoea?"

BILL SPOKE MY LANGUAGE

I knew Bill Hicks before I met him. His was the warm Cornwall to John Arlott's mellow Hampshire as sport on the wireless provided painless schoolboy lessons in geography and painting pictures with words.

Bill was talking football to me, clear and unflustered even when the accumulator started to play tricks, and I admired him all the more on discovering his rich pedigree as a journalist on local and national newspapers.

They were still lauding his pre-war sporting exploits when I joined the Dereham and Fakenham Times payroll in the early 1960s. Such was his legendary prowess in so many fields, a young reporter in town could feel rather inadequate on being confined to extolling the virtues of others.

Bill was too modest to mull over those Norfolk achievements as we met and mardled regularly in recent years. He moved to Cromer at the same time as me, although I had to turn elsewhere for media wisdom in winter as he headed for the sunshine of South Africa and a round or two at Soweto Golf Club.

Bill, who died at 84, did admit to enjoying every stage of his wonderful innings, from Jimmy Dingle's village classroom in the ancient Cornish borough of Launceston to the court of Nelson Mandela. "I'm batting on after tea where so many have had to pull up stumps," he quipped at our final get-together.

He reflected on those heady days of Fleet Street and Sports Report with a benevolence not given to many embroiled in the dog-eat-dog world of bloated personalities, circulation wars and microphone histrionics.

Bill was slow to chide and swift to bless, perfect qualities to take into later work with the Sports Council and as senior lecturer in the journalism department of Harlow Technical College.

As a member of the Queen's English Society he was deeply concerned about the decline in use of our language. The laments of the Prince of Wales and successive secretaries of state for education inspired him to write Maske No Mistake three years ago.

This guide to getting it right, in the classroom, in the office, for all who write for others to read, deserves to stand as a memorial to a gentle man who used words lovingly and carefully, on air, in print or just mardling on Cromer Pier.

I'll miss his ready smile and endless capacity for talking fondly about everyone and everything except himself and his own outstanding career. I'll still hear the warm Cornish tones of W J Hicks as soon as the Sports Report band strikes up.

***

HAIR-RAISING NEWS
A couple of delightful tales from Norman Barrie of Bawburgh to illustrate our special brand of humour.
The first concerned a boy apprentice in a barber's shop at Bungay during the last war. A customer asked the barber if he'd heard the latest.
"What's that then?"
"The jarmans he' got Tobruk"
At home that evening the boy was so quiet his mother asked him: "Is something worrying you?"
"Yes, Mum. Them Jarmans he' got to Brooke – so they might well be here tomorrow".
Then there was an old Norfolk bachelor who lived alone with his dog. When he retired, he was persuaded to have meals-on-wheels. Four years later, old Jimmy said to the delivery lady: "Yew wunt need ter call any more, missus."
"Oh dear. Is there something wrong?"
"Yis – the dawg is dead, an' I like bread 'n' cheese mesself."

***

THEY DEW SAY
Horry: What sort o' clyent wuz yew at skool, bor?
Tom: I dun zakly what Nelson dun ....
Horry: Oh, ar, woss that then?
Tom: I went down in histery!

FOWL PLAY LED TO DIBBLE DISASTER

My shortage of green fingers has been a source of amusement and amazement to family and friends for many years. "How can someone brought up in the heart of the country be such a duffer in the garden?"

A few even laced disdain with suspicions that I had deliberately cultivated this image of utter ineptitude with hoe, rake, fork and spade. Sadly, it came quite naturally after a bad experience with a dibble.

Father and brothers tended our large vegetable patch at the old homestead with enthusiasm and precision. I neither envied nor understood. I had books to read, cricket matches to play, rustic adventures to pursue.

Beans and sprouts were boring old things that came up out of the ground every year. I knew parsnips tasted the better for a good frost and King Edward had as much to do with spuds as expensive cigars – but that was the sum total of my gardening knowledge.

"Scared to get his hands dirty!" and "About as much use as a chocolate teapot!" were among kinder jibes as pricking and planting gave way to watering and weeding and hoeing and admiring. I showed a little interest when it came to picking and eating. Then it was back into the shadows while Mother Nature, father and big brothers got on with it.

The call to dibble duty came unexpectedly one Saturday afternoon when I happened to be the only unemployed boy on the premises. Dad decided I might be better than nothing and sent me to the shed to collect his wretched instrument for making holes. A tray of seed potatoes waited for insertion.

He ushered me ahead, a reluctant trailblazer in short trousers and high dudgeon after being prevented from striking gold down King Solomon's Mines. I could not keep a straight line. One hole was too deep, the next scarcely discernible as Dad's hobnailed boots came crunching towards it.

I could see there were far more potatoes than holes and hit on the bright idea of shortening the distance between them. No one had told me they didn't all have to be planted in the same row or that they needed a certain amount of room to prosper.

My misery plumbed fresh depths about two feet from the chicken run. Just to bring a spot more variety to this rollicking rural scene I poked the dibble through the wire netting. It would not come out again. The hens all rushed to peck and prate at the sudden intruder. Father's reasonable suspicions of fowl play were confirmed all too rapidly. A verdict of misadventure spelt banishment from the blessed plot, a thick ear and a soiled reputation.

The Great Dibble Disaster could have left scars for life. The incident haunted me every time I covered a local horticultural show during my early years as a newspaper reporter. Retirement ceremonies had me scribbling furiously – until the dreaded phrase "spend more time in the garden" brought on palpitations culminating in Dropped Pencil Syndrome.

Home produce continued to flourish, but I wasn't expected to show an interest beyond a hearty appetite and nods of approval at Sunday dinnertime.

Gradually as the seasons melted into each other, I lost that deep sense of guilt over lack of involvement in the annual miracles of sowing and reaping.

I could pass a window box, a greenhouse or a packed allotment without feeling inadequate.

Then, over the compost heap, past the herbaceous border and round the purpose-built canes came The Great Vegetable Plot of 1996. We were going to grow some – and I could do the Percy Thrower impression I'd been hiding under the bushes all these years!

Arguments were quite convincing. I had a bit more time than usual. We had enough room for a little self-sufficiency at the side of the house. I could have a break from raiding the in-laws' supplies of fresh produce and stun them into open-mouthed admiration.

The wife accepted earnest requests not to reawaken horrors from over 40 years ago. She made all the holes and did most of the planting. I demonstrated an uncanny flair for opening brightly-coloured packets and depositing their contents in a fairly straight line. Lack of a chicken run helped me to concentrate.

Well, the plot thickened and I presented the firmest cabbage to my wife on our wedding anniversary. She reciprocated with a colander of freshly-picked broad beans, my favourites.

Call me a sentimental old fool, but I'm hoping to have our very own new potatoes ready for next year's celebration. (I mean next year's crop, of course.) And the perfect riposte will be waiting should mocking tones greet their uprooting...

"Your spuds are on the small side this year..."

"So they might be – but I grow them to fit my mouth, not yours!"

BEYOND THE PAIL
WITH WALLY

When I'm in one of my more puckish moods, I call Litcham "that nice little place not far from my old home village of Beeston."

But there's no hiding genuine affection for a parish where respect for the past is matched by relish for the present. That apparent paradox is explained by the pivotal role played by Litcham Historical Society.

They dig deep, this industrious alliance of native and newcomer, and then gleefully proclaim their discoveries. That puts them at the heart of local social life and strengthens important bonds with the high school. Yesterday feeding tomorrow.

I have been on the receiving end of the Litcham sharing spirit many times, especially with pictorial support for my series of local books. Surrounding villages, including Beeston, are well represented and I've spent many happy hours renewing acquaintance with characters and places I knew as a boy.

In fact, photographs in the village museum go back to 1860, so some of the faces beaming out from mid-Norfolk pastures were sizing up heavenly furrows by the time I made my first expedition to Litcham, a taut little passenger on the back of mother's sturdy bicycle.

I cannot pretend all boyhood trips were orderly and fruitful. When we ran out of ideas in the name of antagonising each other, we Beeston Bruisers would sneak over the border to sort out the Litcham Louts. Well, that was the bloodtingling plan after our council of war.

True to tell, Litcham Common was the scene of countless one-sided contests in between official football fixtures for those with a more grown-up approach to inter-village rivalry.

Our bruises, sniffles, scratches and limps betrayed a long run of away defeats – and could have explained extra rations of respect we brought to our dealings with the Mileham Maulers, Gressenhall Grapplers and Wendling Warriors.

Happily, these rustic exploits were not deemed worthy of inclusion in Litcham, The Short History of a Mid-Norfolk Village, by Eric Puddy, first published in 1957. This goldmine of a book by a local doctor is being given a deserved second innings by Litcham Historical Society at £4.50.

As an honorary member of the society, I got my copy free on a recent visit to the village where scabby-kneed marauders of over 40 years ago are treated more with amused tolerance than as targets for belated retribution.

Dr Puddy also teamed up with the colourful cleric, Noel Boston, to provide us with a much-valued history of East Dereham. (To those who claim I overdo the "East", let me repeat there is a West Dereham in Norfolk. Once you have made the distinction, Dereham will do).

In his foreword to the 1957 Litcham book, Dr Puddy recalled how his search for the past had led to the study of manorial Latin as bad as his own school efforts, and to reading of medieval documents as difficult to decipher as some of his own prescriptions!

He certainly proved local history was anything but dull, the percect cue for his successors as they remind us Litcham once had a thriving market, a tanning industry, a cock-pit, a racecourse, a fire brigade, village stocks and a local concert party called The Litcham Mirthquakes.

A sombre Beeston echo from May 29, 1872 – "The tower of the church was struck by lightning. The Litcham fire engine was taken into the church but the molten lead and burning timbers fell so rapidly that nothing could be done, and the tower was entirely destroyed."

Manorial courts, Litcham Hall – known as Pill Hall because of the surgeons who lived there – the Bull Inn, its oldest parts going back to the 15th century, and Litcham Common nature reserve are just a few of the other items demanding close attention.

Let me end my latest short stroll around Litcham with this potent little extract from the Puddy journey up to 1957.

"At the appointed times, the night soil cart could be heard rumbling up the street, lit by an old-fashioned candle-lantern swinging from the outside shaft. The rumbling of the wheels would cease, and within seconds arose the snoring of Wally Feeke's old mule.

"Pails clanked, the midnight air became less ambient, the mule woke with a start and moved along to the next cottage as in a fantasy."

When I get round to writing the Norfolk version of "under Milk Wood", Wally Feeke will have a starring role. I might call it "Beyond The Pail".

RUSTIC RIB-TICKLERS IN CORONATION MILK

It started when the chap on the farm called the new mechanical monster a concubine harvester. We gave him free electrocution lessons.

Then a local preacher told us Moses collected the Ten Commandments on Mount Cyanide. And we think he said Salome danced in front of Harrods.

A boy in my class at school definitely wrote Ali Baba as saying that you were somewhere else when you were there – and proving it. Only the other day I heard an old Norfolk worthy suggest a lot of people go to Walsingham where they throw that incest about...

Rustic malapropisms, schoolboy groaners, family foibles (or at least the ones Aesop didn't use), tips of the slongue and priceless Norfolkisms – I've collected a big crop over the years.

With the festive season around the corner, and happy gatherings bound to demand examples of homespun humour as an anecdote – sorry – antidote for too much turkey and telly, let me share a few favourites.

I know Walter Gabriel's old granny used to come out with some rum sayings, and every Norfolk village must have had her equivalent when I was a lad. They were at their best when describing ailments, ranging from haricot veins to multiplication of the bowels.

"They reckon our blood's med up o'two kinds of corkscrews – red corkscrews an' white ones" and "She had ter hev sum o' them contradictive pills" still make me chuckle. As does the famous notice in a country doctor's surgery – "No torkin' – and hev yer simptums riddy."

There was nothing medical about the ceremony as far as I know, but many a new Norfolk vicar was induced before being told what time to celebrate Holy Commotion. The old churchwarden had the perfect answer when asked by a newcomer if they had matins in the church. "No, we hev lino ryte up ter the altar!"

The village shop was another rich source of instant humour, some of it off the top shelf reserved for regular packages. Old Harry only once had to ask for a roll of Anthrax and a legend was born. Edith's girl needed but a single order for some of that Coronation milk to go on tinned peaches and her place in local folklore was assured. Young Billy would be destined for stardom as soon as he admitted to listening to the fizz of them Helter-Skelter tablets in the glass.

Several rounds of chortling down at The Eradicated Coypu as one regular said he was ready to throw his hat into the political marina as soon as they called local election time, and another urged all right-minded customers to sign his partition against them triculated lorries thundering through the parish.

Landlord joins in the spirit by asking who wants to see the holiday snaps he took with a new Paranoid camera, while his wife wonders if the Morris dancers calling next week will reveal the secrets of their futility rites.

I recall an old salt at Gorleston listening for one of them macaroons to launch the lifeboat. I heard a dear old girl at Yarmouth describe how those indecency bombs had scared her during the war. I noted how a Caister fisherman was convinced herrings went about the sea in shawls.

A Fakenham man told me he had seen a real Lord wearing a scarlet robe trimmed with vermins. When his sister got excited – that's the Fakenham man who could paint wonderful pictures with words – she was overcome with emulsion. Probably to the extent of going into the shop to ask for a pint of semi-skilled milk.

Little blasts from notebooks past. And I'm still jotting down little gems. Like the woman who always gets her facts and names slightly muddled. "Didn't Stanley Matthews marry one of them Andrews Sisters? Tell you my favourite film star – Eddie Nelson. They asked me if I like Delius. I told them... I've got all her recipes."

There's fun to be had with comparatively new words and ideas. Many a Norfolk computer travels into the city for work each day. I was reliably informed that an 87-year-old retired farmworker, yet to surf the Internet, had started a villaganti movement near Reepham. I approached with caution. He told me it was quite simple. He lived in the village. He was anti newcomers. And nosey media people.

Let me wind up with a classic from the Norfolk village classroom.

The teacher explained that "excavate" meant "to hollow out". "Now," she said, "I would like a sentence using the word 'excavate'."

Up shot Charlie's hand. "Please, Miss... I dropped a big ole weight on my dad's toe and he excavated."

PIER'S THE PLACE FOR CROMER PRIDE

One of the characters in Jane Austen's Emma, first published in 1816, says: "Perry was a week in Cromer once, and he holds it to be the best of all the sea-bathing places. A fine open sea, he says, and very pure air."

Now, I don't work for the local tourist board and nor do I have aspirations in that direction, but I reckon old Perry's seaside sentiments could be taken down, dusted and used in evidence 180 years later.

Jane Austen is back in fashion after lavish film and television productions of her novels. Cromer never goes out of fashion, because it pays no heed to trends or slick tricks of the holiday trade.

I love Cromer at this time of year if skies are clear and the wind not too lazy to go round you. Then the pier assumes its dominant role of luring bit-part players on to centre-stage. Grand scenery, including the town tumbling towards you if the church lets go, can inspire summer thoughts in winter:

Waves patrol below
Hands pump above
Slap and clap
Stage tests water
With toes in the sea

A platform for anglers dotted round the Pavilion Theatre. A haven for strollers who relish the old Norfolk trick of having one foot on land and the other in the sea. There's room to think. And there's always the prospect of serious action down the slipway.

Lifeboat stabled just
Beyond the footlights
Does old Blogg
Take a bow
On stormy nights?

I recall how the dramatic events of November, 1993, left me marooned and often miserable. The pier was sliced in half by a runaway barge and became one of the area's leading tourist "attractions" before a new holiday season beckoned with the official reopening six months later. How I missed my little outings to the end of the pier, especially when I felt fairly close to the end of my tether!

No doubt many experienced similar withdrawal symptoms in

1940 when it was decided to blow up the central portion of the pier to prevent any invading troops having easy access to the town.

Local people were warned demolition would take place at noon on a particular Saturday and advised to open their windows to lessen damage from the blast. High noon came and went. Nothing happened. Many residents closed their windows, only to regret it when at about four o'clock there was an almighty explosion. Debris shattered windows and damaged property.

Then it dawned on the demolition brigade that the lifeboat crew couldn't get down to the lifeboat shed. "Ha, well done Wilson – I was wondering who would be the first to notice that little problem" said Cromer's answer to Captain Mainwaring. Temporary planking went over the hole. In dark and wet conditions the crew must have been in greater danger going across that gap than they were in the churning sea.

The savage 1953 floods also took their toll, but the present Cromer pier must now be ready for anything else fate can throw at it before centenary celebrations in 2001.

The Hunstanton pier I used regularly as a child on Sunday School outings was destroyed by storms in January 1978. Happily there are still good companions for Cromer along our coastline at Yarmouth, Gorleston, Lowestoft, Southwold and Felixstowe.

I got close to the Britannia and Wellington piers at Yarmouth during my days on the local newspaper in the mid-1960s. Rubbing shoulders with showbusiness stars was a big pull, although I did come to see the Brit in a different light when Ralph Eustace Sherwin White, colourful chief reporter on the Yarmouth Mercury, described it thus in his Scout column: "Like Neptune's giant frying-pan stretching into the sea."

Lowestoft looked set to have a partner for the South Pier at the end of the last century. Indeed, the Duke of Cambridge cut the first turf in connection with the North Pier project in 1899, but the £60,000 idea sank without trace. Still, the Claremont Pier was built in 1903 by the Coast Development Corporation to serve as a stopping place for the Belle steamers between London and Yarmouth.

I can't see many new schemes finding favour towards the end of this century – or at the start of the next one. All the more reason, then, to savour these marvellous facilities for all seasons:

End of the pier where
An era lives on
Out of curiosity
And affection
For old-fashioned ways.

YANKS FOR ALL
THE MEMORIES

Dinner with the Americans was an enlightening experience, even though I am more used to catching up with gossip from Beeston and Mileham rather than the Bronx and Manhattan.

My wife was impressed at the way I let conversation flow, cutting down drastically on my normal rations of interruptions and asides. Being asked if I were a professor proved both flattering and shrewd.

Flattering because I have never attracted such an educated guess before. Shrewd because the rest of the table were six subjects ahead of me by the time I got over the shock. An object lesson in keeping a notoriously loquacious local in check.

They knew my chance would arrive later when the assembled company had to pay attention and listen to me saluting them for coming to one of the best places in the world. Coming back, in many cases, to refresh the deep roots of their affection.

This was a welcoming dinner for a reunion of Americans based at Watton during the last war with the Third Strategic Air Depot, the largest B-24 Liberator maintenance and supply facility in military history.

Ken and Jan Godfrey, of Carbrooke, near Watton, have been organising these reunions for many years, and they are extremely wary of suggesting the end of the nostalgic runway could be nigh. Just when it looks as if interest may be tailing off, another trip is keenly supported.

I wasn't entirely out of my depth on an occasion alive with wartime memories. For a start there was my introduction to Glenn Miller. True, I was barely six months into my Norfolk stride when the great bandleader led his musicians into a giant hangar about a mile from my old homestead at Beeston.

Our local airfield, home to the 392nd Bomb Group, was carved out of farmland between Beeston and Wendling, so both villages can stake a claim to a slice of aviation and showbusiness history. Five B-24s landed on August 25, 1944, and unloaded Glenn Miller's Band to entertain US servicemen and their new-found friends. A full house of 3000 quickly got in the mood.

I often wondered why my green pram seemed to possess a swaying mind of its own that afternoon as I gurgled, smiled and kicked my legs in the air. Mother put it down to wind and impatience for the next round of refreshments, but I know now it must have been the strains of beautiful music carried across the meadows.

Come to think of it, a chuck under the chin at teatime was accompanied by what sounded uncannily like an impromptu rendition of Chattanooga Choo Choo.

Glenn Miller's engagements of the previous week had included concerts at Attlebridge and the Samson and Hercules Ballroom in Norwich. Following their appearance on my old home patch, the band immediately flew off to regale the 388th Bomb Group at Knettishall in West Suffolk.

After dinner they played to a crowd of 7000 in a hangar so cold that some of the musicians, including maestro Miller, played with gloves on. August hospitality at Beeston was on the slightly warmer side.

I was assured at the reunion dinner that Americans don't mind stories against themselves when it comes to reflections on the friendly invasion. There's a large selection, most of them culminating in the old Norfolk boy taking the main honours just when he seems to be beaten. Two of my favourites from this department...

A couple of American servicemen were waiting for a train. They kept on telling the ancient Norfolk porter they had bigger and faster trains back home. They were about to elaborate when a fast train to Yarmouth raced through, hauled by a Britannia class locomotive. "Gee, buddy, what was that?" asked one of the Americans.

"Oh," said the porter, "That wuz old Tom dewin' a bit o'shuntin'!"

Then there was old George showing an American round the village.

"Thass our chatch. Took nigh on twetty year ter bild few sentries ago," he said.

"Wall, buddy, I guess in Texas we could erect one in five," the American answered.

Slightly miffed, George then pointed out the new council school. "Wot bowt that, then? Only took nine munth ter bild that."

"Gee, I reckon back home we erect a school in six months at most."

They turned a corner. there stood the village hall.

"Say, buddy, what's that building?"

"Dunno," said George without batting an eyelid. "That wunt there when I cum ter wak this mornin'."

P.C. BRIAN – LIGHTHOUSE OF THE LAW

Perhaps the warmest tribute I can pay Cromer's community-loving policeman is to admit I had to be reminded of his surname. PC Brian Adkins, a veritable lighthouse of the law at well over 6ft, died suddenly just a few months before retirement.

He was an exceptional officer who stayed true to old-fashioned virtues in an increasingly cynical world. If his size made him conspicuous, his smile still remained his most arresting feature.

I have no idea if he had the chance to climb the promotion ladder but spurned it in favour of sticking to the Norfolk coastal beat. I don't know if his plain approach to the job with all its growing demands and pressures, met with the general approval of working colleagues and superiors.

I am certain he took all blandishments and well-meant advice in his ample stride – and then carried on doing it his way. PC Brian, as he was known to folk of all ages, did as much as he could to fill the vast gap between an era of unbridled respect for the local bobby and an age of flagrant disregard for the sanctity of law and order.

His links with local schools, as a governor, liaison officer and especially in connection with cycling proficiency tests and road safety, gave him the chance to drop little seeds along paths leading to a tough old world waiting round the corner.

He didn't preach or patronise, and pupils, parents and teachers nodded and smiled their thanks. His presence was never intimidating in the classroom, but nor were youngsters allowed to forget the important bond between affection and regard. PC Brian would let you try on his helmet as long as you appreciated what it stood for.

He took me "into custody" a couple of years ago, pulling up to offer a lift into Norwich. My arrival at work in a police car prompted quizzical glances and sly nudges as he opened the door an wagged an admonishing finger under my nose...

On a crisp morning we chatted about the changing face of society. I drew comparisons between the Norfolk of my boyhood, when policemen were feared, revered and seemingly always approaching on an ominously steady bicycle, and the current scene littered with wailing sirens, high-speed chases, violent crimes and contempt for the very basics of decency and honesty.

PC Brian suggested this was part of the price Norfolk had to pay for "catching up" with the rest of the world. Some villains would travel remarkably long distances to do a job, picking on small, quiet places often ill-prepared for such professional visits. Total indifference to people and property was born largely out of easier access to and from more remote areas for the new, super-mobile criminal classes.

Even so, he warned me not simply to see yesterday full of rosy-cheeked apple-scrumpers and rusty bikes without lights and today crammed with drug barons, armed robbers and street muggers.

Yes, there was more open aggression and malice, and authority had to endure sneering abuse from youngsters who knew their "rights". But human strengths and weaknesses came out in any social climate, and it was important to keep faith with the forces of good in a difficult time.

"That's one of the reasons I became a policeman, and that is why I spend so much of my spare time with youngsters. You can't win 'em all, but you can cut down the odds against them going off the tracks."

PC Brian summed himself up as "a walker, a talker and a rattler of doors." He believed policemen were at their most effective when they were seen and heard among the people they served.

His death at 49 has robbed North Norfolk of a caring and colourful character who was just as concerned about keeping youngsters on the straight and narrow as he was about nabbing those who fell away.

I once heard him described – well out of earshot as he strolled through town – as "a left-over from Dock Green." He would have taken that as a compliment, saluted and reminded a crime-obsessed society that prevention is still better than detention.

***

WORTH A TRY
An old tradesman in a Norfolk town was a notoriously bad payer and none too scrupulous in his business dealings.
His frequent appearances in the county court led the judge on one occasion to ask if he did not think "honesty is the best policy"?
To this the old tradesman instantly relied: "Dunno, yer honour – I hent never tried it!"

NOSTALGIA RULES

Byways researchers have been tuning in to the wonderful world of wireless on recent local travels, accumulating memories that really are the cat's whiskers.

They received an excellent reception in over 250 villages with inquiries about favourite radio programmes, old and new. Nostalgia ruled the airwaves in many places and there were examples of the personality cult being taken to extremes – such as at Woganhall St Germans and Hockwold-cum-Rob Wilton.

Even so, the survey revealed deep and lasting affection for certain shows and characters making a mark well before the cultural revolution spawned by the likes of Chris Evans and Danny Baker.

This week's Top 10 will be repeated on the Home Service on Friday evening:

1. Round the Horning
2. Down Your Weybourne
3. Much Binding in the Marsham
4. Mrs Bale's Diary
5. Dick Barton Turf
6. Desert Island Diss
7. Lyng Something Simple
8. Have a Hoe
9. Brooke at Bedtime
10. Brain of Fritton

***

NOT FOR SALE
An old Norfolk farmer retired and a big crowd attended the sale of cattle, machinery and vehicles.
Everything was sold except one brightly-painted farm wagon.
"Woss the idea, Horry?" asked several visitors. "Arn't yew goin' ter sell that wagon?"
"No," replied the farmer. "Rekun I'll keep that ole wagon a bit longer. I'd feel sort o' lorst if I hent got noffin ter lend a neighbour at harvest time!"

HEDGEROW HARVEST

If you are searching for a spot of constancy in our ever-changing world, head for the hedgerow.

Picking blackberries proves that some things simply do not change. I have been raiding Mother Nature's larder for well over 40 years, and she is still dishing out the same old rewards and reminders.

Visions of cosy Sunday teas around the blazing hearth must be tempered with acceptance of scratches, stings, bites, stains and cuts on the way.

The biggest and juiciest fruit are still a tantalising inch or two from your fingertips. Torn trousers, plucked pullovers and real thorns in the side are predictable prices to pay for overreaching ambition.

Our family raiding party to the Beckhams, Bodham, Baconsthorpe and beyond confirmed three other facts of blackberry-picking life. Growing boys still eat far more than they collect. Mothers still get on with the job while fathers keep on reciting hedgerow adventures from long ago.

You all spot the biggest and best clusters just waiting to fall into your basket while you are heading home. But that's quite enough for another year.

***

TALKING SHOP
Back in the 1930s, a shopkeeper in a remote Norfolk village kept a commercial traveller waiting.

The only assistant was a young girl who, standing on a stool to reach a tine of peas, dislodged some others. One crashed on to the commercial traveller's head.

Luckily, he was wearing a hard, black hat. It was knocked over his eyes.

To be so ill-used while waiting patiently for orders was bad enough. But the poor man's humiliation was complete as the shopkeeper snapped: "Hey, dew yew be careful, Daphne – that might he' bin a customer!"

LITTLE TROSHING SET TO SLAY DRAGONS

Little Troshing (also incorporating the decayed parishes of Barleysele and Bindertwine) is ready to take on the dragons of rural destruction!

That's the clarion call after a lively but well-mannered St George's Day meeting in this Norfolk hamlet of 56 souls. They offered a cautious welcome to revelations that humanity is set to become a predominantly urban species for the first time in its two-million-year history.

"By the end of the century more people will be living in towns and cities than in the countryside. That must have repercussions from Bombay to Brisley," suggested Miss Harper as she chaired the get-together in the William Morris Memorial Lounge at the Old rectory. She made a mental note to buy new wallpaper.

Parish council chairman and retired dentist Amos Horkey said it was excellent news because he didn't like noise, pollution, crowds, poverty, Sunday trading, buskers, beggars and traffic wardens.

Billy Windham, always ready to entertain an alternative point of view after many years as a traffic warden in Chelmsford, agreed it was excellent news because he didn't go a bundle on noise, pollution, crowds, poverty, Sunday trading, buskers, beggars and former dentists.

After a break for refreshments in the Dante Gabriel Rosetti Memorial Kitchen retired bank manager Ernest Dough-Jones said he felt it incumbent upon him to proffer a serious point they were in danger of overlooking in their search for self-preservation.

He allayed fears of yet another lecture on the merits of a single currency and asked his fellow Arcadians if they had taken on board the distinct possibility that a dramatic rise in the urban population might lead to inordinate burdens on those who had the good sense to avail themselves of a country residence...

"What are you trying to say?" snapped retired advertising consultant Percy Smuckerling.

"He means there'll be millions more of the crafty beggars looking for an escape to places just like this!" hinted Amos Horkey.

"Thank goodness for the structure plan and the village envelope!" enthused Miss Harper. Thirteen parishioners thought she meant another collection was about to be taken up for repairs to the Reading Room and hunted frantically for small change.

"I propose we call an emergency session of the Federation Against Rural Turbulence," said Billy Windham. He volunteered to go on his bike to rouse the good people of the sleepy neighbouring parishes of Lower Dodman, Upper Muckwash and Puckaterry Parva. As hands shot up in favour he made a mental note to buy a puncture-mending outfit.

Over coffee in the Mary Mitford Memorial Conservatory it was firmly agreed that only by standing shoulder to shoulder could Norfolk's small communities repel the potential threat posed by Urban Man on the cusp of the Millennium.

Percy Smuckerling cleared his throat and pronounced: "Image is the real problem, y'know. Television, cinema, books and all those blasted colour supplements... they're to blame."

No one contradicted, so he charged on.

"They think we live on Cold Comfort Farm, pick the Darling Buds of May all year round and do our bit for public transport by making Love on a Branch Line. They assume our pigs talk and they know all our cows are mad. They just love our quaint little ways and can't wait to find dear old Miss Marple solving murders over tinkling teacups at the rectory. Oh, no offence meant, Miss Harper..."

She gave him a businesslike look and made a mental note to organise a village pageant next St George's Day.

"Very good, Sir Percy. If we can get you down from that white charger for a moment you could play an important role in keeping the advancing hordes at bay. This is no time to delve too deeply into possible reasons for your arrival amongst us at the height of the property boom. Let me just thank you in advance for a most generous contribution to the Reading Room repair fund."

Percy Smuckerling knew Miss Harper was about to sound like that dratted Irish comedian.

"Come here, Sir Percy, there's more. We would like you to prepare one of those smart video presentations to dispel a few myths about village life. We can send it to all the tourist boards, John Craven and that nice man with the sheepdogs. "Sheer Hell In the Sticks" makes a useful working title and I'm sure Granny Pinkerton will be only too pleased to pose for you in her little listed building covered in ivy at the top of her garden..."

Percy Smuckerling left quietly through the John Ruskin Memorial Orchard. He made a mental note to find out more about rural deprivation.

And to keep off high horses when Miss Harper was around.

OVER THE BORDER
A SOUND IDEA

A Suffolk sanctuary hemmed in by the golden stubble of another harvest home nurtured only a few grains of guilt at leaving my own backyard for a couple of weeks.

We were housed a few miles over the border and this was a repeat journey down lanes waiting for blackberries to ripen and fields to change colour.

Elder son had decided to leaven the pioneering spirit as soon as he spied Beccles church across the marshes. "We're abroad again!" he cried with a chuckle designed to forestall Dad's usual sermon on marvels left behind.

I exacted subtle revenge with a couple of nifty Norfolk crawlers at a critical time in the second Orchard Test Match, but this holiday will be remembered for a shortage of references to withdrawal symptoms, passport controls and funny old men set in their ways.

Our idyllic base inspired a competition based on the variety of sounds when wind and rain allowed. I saw nothing nasty in the woodshed but there were enough rattles, rustles and shuffles to put Cold Comfort Farm in the shade.

Some noises were easy to identify – owls hooting away any pretence to subterfuge as they left the eaves in the small hours – but the pet rabbit's rhythmic beat on the hutch floor provoked a lengthy nocturnal search for a puckish woodpecker or bats wearing clogs.

Our main contest centred on coming up with collective nouns for creatures providing a vibrant background chorus for this break in the country. A "coocophony" of plump pigeons took main honours each morning at first light, while a chortle of pheasants, a scatter of moorhens and a bounce of grey squirrels made useful supporting acts.

Dragonflies trying to do impressions of helicopters in Apocalypse Now and wasps turning every windfall into a lottery are among those forced to wait for a welcome to nature's showbiz bill

We explored other lanes, analysed other sounds and watched the same harvest nearing completion. Norman Scarfe's lines in The Suffolk Landscape took on renewed appeal and significance: "In Suffolk the fields are never far off. However increasingly town-moulded all the upbringing of Suffolk people may be the fields spread round us throughout our lives.

"We cannot ride through them without being conscious, if only out of the corner of our eyes, of their daily response to the seasons, their extraordinary fertility and their endless diversity of shape and pattern."

We renewed acquaintance with the light and splendour of Blythburgh church at the head of an estuary, above marsh and heath, and moved on uplifted to find the fascinating church within a church at Covehithe.

The old building, now in ruins, went up early in the 15th century. When it became clear it was much too large, with maintenance costs way beyond the means of a small community, permission was granted in 1672 to build the small church out of materials from the original structure. Ecclesiastical recycling at its best.

In 1974 the ruins were transferred to the Redundant Churches Fund, which has carried out repairs on the arches and the old tower, so long a guide to shipping.

As the wind blew in from the sea and through tall, long walls we made tracks for Wrentham Village Hall where Covehithe's story features as part of a splendid local history exhibition.

A return visit to Framlingham Castle coincided with a dramatic storm. Consolation for sitting in the car park was in instant son-et-luminere production as lightning forked over the Plantagenet towers and thunder crashed round the Tudor brick chimneys which stand somewhat precariously on them.

Bungay Castle was bathed in sunshine as we called on friends who live next door to Roger Bigod's ruined masterpiece.

Only a matter of yards from town on market day, but we found real peace and calm in a cottage garden.

Finally, a tip on how to find a parking space in Southwold in summer. Make your approach at teatime after a spell of heavy rain and there is an even chance of coming across a gap fairly close to shops and seafront.

When Southwold is heaving with people and cars I need to think twice about accepting a Suffolk friend's suggestion that it is "simply Cromer with an A-level."

MAKE A NOISE TO PROTECT PEACE

An old Norfolk saying I just made up suggests progress is in order so long as it doesn't change anything. That crafty contradiction presents itself in the face of current debates about the information revolution, road building cuts and rural tranquility. Hi-tech, highways and low decibels.

I can't help wondering how many of those spitting blood at our so-called condemnation to life in the slow lane heaved sighs of regret over the startling news that our peace and quiet have been shattered by development, new roads and increasing traffic.

Running with the hare and chasing with the hounds has become a fashionable pastime in recent years, especially among those who talk about striking a balance long after that balance has been lost.

"Maximising economic advantages without harming the environment" was on the Broadland agenda while pollution, overcrowding, greed and complacency were taking their tragic toll on one of Europe's most important wetlands.

"Encouraging people to come without ruining the very things they come for" was a tantalising text for tourist chiefs well before sensible ideas like the North Norfolk Coast Project were set up in the name of beauty's survival.

"The countryside needs tourism as much as tourism needs the countryside" is the latest handy slogan adopted by bodies with vested interests in making the most of areas still managing to rub shoulders with peace and quiet.

I am not advocating an end to all road improvements – you probably have your own favourite potholes needing urgent attention – but surely less traffic and better driving must come higher on the list of priorities as Norfolk tries to work out where it is going towards the end of the century.

New roads generate more traffic. "Better communications" widen commuter areas – ask places like Buckinghamshire for proof – and there are some well-respected voices raised against the long, loud argument that Norfolk will lose out economically through poor roads.

After all, if it were easier for Norfolk to distribute goods in the Midlands, would it not follow that the Midlands could distribute goods to Norfolk more readily? Could that not lead to more redundancies rather than the creation of more jobs? And how come we were chugging along quite nicely before the recession despite those horrible highways?

Communities under siege from thundering vehicles must accept that a bypass simply shoves the problems elsewhere, destroying another slice of landscape with the prospect of a few more filling stations, warehouses, supermarkets and refreshment havens. (And a bypass for the bypass...)

Another awkward question that shouldn't be dodged. How many people moaning at Long Stratton about the delay over their bypass took the slightest notice as the village in particular and the area in general turned into Commuterbland.?

If only campaigns for better public transport could attract the same brand of aggression and levels of publicity stoked up by the roads lobby! If only those who claim to appreciate the value of tranquility made a bit more noise about protecting it!

All too often we wait for grim statistics before shaking a fist at the reasons behind them. I've got a little list in case there's some you missed...

About 11,000 hectares (27,000 acres) of land are swallowed up for building each year in this country. By 2050, predicts the Council for the Protection of Rural England, one fifth of the land area of England will be urban.

Traffic flows are set to increase by at least 25 per cent over the next 20 years. More than 20,000 commuters drive into Norwich every morning and out again at night. Some 75,000 other vehicles arrive daily on the city outskirts.

Almost 60 per cent of Norfolk's hedges were removed between 1964 and 1981 and 73 per cent of grassland has disappeared since 1946. Add all the problems surrounding our ancient woodland, river valleys, heathland, Areas of Outstanding Natural Beauty and Sites of Special Scientific Interest and you have some idea why peace and quiet are in such short supply.

We were told a few days ago that in this region alone a quiet area more than 25 times the size of Norwich has been lost since the 1960s, with rural Norfolk particularly at risk. Lady Walpole, chairman of the Norfolk Society, rightly emphasised the point: "Because the loss of tranquility is creeping and insidious it is perhaps difficult to fully appreciate."

I say the most telling way of measuring that loss is to make your own list of places you have used simply to relax and soak up the silence. How many of those havens are still there? And how fearful are you that the remnants can survive the rest of the century?

Countryman-writer Adrian Bell graced this paper in 1956 with these sentiments: "How rare a thing is silence; how few in the world today are so placed that they can hear nothing. We have everything – from television to wrapped bread in slices – everything but this; that on an evening in May a man may experience that complex murmur which is nature falling asleep, without the crooning of someone's radio or the explosion of motor engines."

Even rarer 40 years on as the need to escape from noise and congestion is heightened by Norfolk's insistence on doing the same as everywhere else instead of dewin' diffrunt.

Thankfully, if you listen long enough you can hear the still, small voice suggesting better communication is just as much about Paths to Tranquility as Roads to Prosperity.

HEART UNDER STRAIN

All Norfolk towns are tatty round the edges as ribbon development continues to gnaw away precious character and space.

Recent visits to Fakenham, Sheringham, Swaffham, North Walsham and Wymondham simply underlined a growing impression that sprawl is now accepted as inevitable.

Long Stratton and Mundesley may call themselves villages, but they betray many of the symptoms of towns losing track of once-distinctive shape and identity. They have put on too much weight too quickly along with others like Mattishall and Mulbarton. We who remember trimmer figures shake our heads in deep disappointment.

But I save my biggest sighs for Dereham, in serious danger of suffering cardiac arrest at the very heart of Norfolk.

Perhaps my views are coloured by fond memories of schoolboy escapades round the shops and market, fun of the harvest fair and Saturday night dance sessions at the Sunshine Floor, along with three happy years on the local newspaper reporting rounds in the early 1960s.

Dereham was the lively but relatively homely centre of my Norfolk world. Now I find it depressing, especially after dark. Feelings of foreboding have been reinforced by news that security cameras are planned to combat vandalism at the parish church.

Passing through the other evening, I squirmed again at the way Dereham staggers into Toftwood on a trail of new homes squeezed among factories and stores, a jumble of bollards, lights, lines of parked vehicles and enough street furniture to cover the Neatherd Moor several times.

I cannot believe Dereham is as pleasant a place to live or work in as it was 30 years ago. I feel no welcome as an occasional visitor. Yet there are influential figures anxious for more.

The town has been labelled as a centre for major concentration of new growth under the Norfolk Structure Plan review. One member of the town council did have the courage to object. Tony Park claimed that what they were voting for would destroy the nature of Dereham.

Mr Park was taken to task by veteran councillor Les Potter who has helped fashion more far-reaching decisions in this county than I have had warm dinners. He accused his colleague of displaying a "little island" mentality.

Well, better a pleasant little island than a grubby ocean of excessive development. That may sound like plaintive cry from the battlements of Fortress Norfolk – but there is too much clear evidence of beleaguered county to ignore it.

As wizards of technology can confuse information with knowledge, so too many of our councillors are apt to mistake expansion for progress. And places like dear old Dereham suffer.

***

PAYING HIM BACK
Old Nathan Nobbs, the village builder employing six local men, was a bit of a skinflint. He agreed to pay them for Christmas Day but said if they wanted Boxing Day off it would be without pay.
When he arrived at the yard on Boxing Day morning none of the men had turned up. But he found a large notice pinned to the gate:"Owing ter bizness being slack, Nathan Nobbs, builder of this parish, hev been unable to pay his men for thar Boxing Day holiday. It is hoped that by next autumn trade will hev improved so he kin pay 'em for the two minnits' silence on Armistice Day."

SIZE NEED NOT KILL VILLAGE SPIRIT

Larger Norfolk villages have to tolerate plenty of rude remarks. I know. I've made enough on my rounds in recent years, "bloated dormitory", "sprawling mess" and "where am I?" among the more flattering.

Even people who live in these fast-expanding places accept they are doing a fair impression of suburbia in terms of appearance, especially where new estates have swallowed up whole fields and increased traffic has put a tremble in the trellis.

The fact this county still boasts a sufficient number of small, pretty and lively villages to satisfy calendar photographers and the holiday brochure brigade simply underlines the dilemma facing bigger brethren.

They may have better facilities – thriving school, two pubs, row of shops, new community centre, restaurant and takeaway, garage with convenience store, doctor's surgery – but is there a real community heart beating away?

I felt bold enough to take that question on recent travels to Rackheath and Swanton Morley.

It was carnival time in both places, one trying hard to keep a bit of daylight between the village and the fringes of Norwich, the other striving to stay free of East Dereham's growing tentacles.

The time it took Rackheath's procession of floats to parade from the parish church to the playing field, albeit at a stately pace, acted as a perfect reminder of the village's exceptional size.

A resident of more than half-a-century, wearing enough greasepaint to avoid instant recognition, admitted he knew few of the people he was waving to along the route.

But the very fact they had come out on a Sunday morning to salute all the hard work that had gone into tricolating the floats gave him a warm feeling he didn't get very often.

The same sort of appreciative murmurings accompanied a Saturday teatime parade at Swanton Morley towards the gala opening of the new village hall. "They can't all be thumbing a lift!" chuckled one of the organisers, suggesting this show of public interest and support represented a fair measure of local involvement in local affairs.

Its a long way from one end of Swanton Morley to the other and, as in many other Norfolk communities asked to take a considerable development in recent years, opinion is divided over the benefits of growth.

"Plenty big enough now we're here; we agree with you about pulling the drawbridge." said one Home Counties voice, initially teasing but leaving the door open for a serious chat.

"We got used to newcomers with the RAF here all those years, and they were kind to the older people. Now the Army's moving in, so we have to get on with them." The native's smile hinted at a mixture of cheerful resignation and tactful co-operation.

Swanton Morley's new village hall, adventurous in design but with work to do in the name of better acoustics, is a symbol of an expanding community's commitment to finding a clear voice, a focal point to nurture well beyond the usual "there if you want it" philosophy.

As I said before cutting the ribbon to a fresh era, one of the main hopes for a revival of the "old-fashioned" feeling of belonging in villages of all shapes and sizes is regular get-togethers of people of all ages and interests.

The village hall, properly run and genuinely welcoming, can help reduce vandalism, isolation and fear in places where these afflictions have grown with the population.

Yes, I caught Rackheath and Swanton Morley on good days. They were going out of their way to prove that while bigger may not be beautiful, there is no reason why it shouldn't spell care and provision.

***

PLAY IT AGAIN
I enjoy the glorious predictabilities of life. For instance, you know when you catch one foot in front of the other and nearly fall over, some bright spark will ask: "Enjoy your trip?"
You offer to buy a drink for your friends in the pub, and they both ask the landlord if he saw that pig flying over the bar.
"How did City get on?" "They dew nil-nil." "What was the score at half-time?" Little gems on regular display.
Returning from a pleasant trip to the Waveney Valley the other Sunday, I made a bet with myself as it was agreed we would make our way back via Reedham Ferry.
I was over a minute out. It took a mere 17 seconds for one of our party to ask the ferryman if the duty-free shop was open. We sniggered. His smile was a mixture of pity and benevolence.
I suppose the time to worry is when he offers to dip your lights.

THE OLD QUEST FOR A STRAIGHT FURROW

I stood on the headlands watching man and machine in the old quest for a straight furrow.

A froth of seagulls at the blade waiting for rich pickings from the chocolate-brown soil. The sun, a pale silver disc overhead, suddenly found courage to charm away a curling mist.

"A straight furrow is the tribute that Agriculture pays to Art. There is virtue in a straight line, which calls for concentration and skill. Where this is skill there is art..."

I looked him up when I got home, that Norfolk ploughing picture turning my day into a strange mixture of confession and celebration. John Stewart Collis was a scholar who became a farm labourer during the last war.

His experiences inspired the book The Worm Forgives The Plough, now widely regarded as a classic. But he was sadly neglected during the years he was learning to plough a straight furrow. He worked on farms in Sussex and Dorset, writing down what had happened at the end of each day to give the pages their authenticity and vividness.

"When the dusk fell and I could go on no longer, I often caught the sharp whiff of smell coming from the upturned earth. Scent is a mighty marvel. What it is I do not know. But I knew what this smell was, which is the most intoxicating of all. It was – fertility. It is life itself coming across to me in pure sensation – the odour of eternal resurrection from the dead."

I confess to sheer envy. I want to feel like that, and find the powers to say so, next time I linger to watch the gulls and history following the plough.

I celebrate this November reunion with another master of rural literature, worthy of a seat at "fourses" time alongside the likes of Adrian Bell and Henry Williamson. Working writers who had to scrub the mud from their hands before picking up the evening pen.

No great literary pretensions about The Memoirs of Josiah Sage, but he and other stalwarts of the agricultural workers' union ploughed enough straight furrows with their sweat and sacrifice to earn our constant admiration.

Published in 1951, this little volume about big men was sent to me by Margaret Loveday of Harleston. Josiah, or "Comrade Joe" as his friends came to call him, was born in Kenninghall. He wrote these memoirs at 81 as one of the very few people to remember the days when the revered Joseph Arch led and organised the agricultural workers.

"Josiah was my father-in-law's great uncle. A wiry old boy, he could still jump a six-foot ditch at the age of 80. He ended his days in the Burston-Winfarthing area, and his wife was secretary to George Edwards, the MP," says Margaret.

Josiah's father was one of the key local figures in Arch's union, which ceased to exist in 1896. Josiah was among those who pioneered the rebirth of agricultural trade unionism 10 years later and was a delegate at the North Walsham conference which marked the beginning of the NUAW.

I was most intrigued to discover another George Edwards in a gallery of outstanding characters featured by Josiah Sage.

"It is not the George Edwards who became famous for his work in founding the present NUAW that I want to write about here, for by a coincidence we had a George Edwards at Kenninghall in the labour movement long before and there was no family connection between them.

"He was a man of many parts, a noted bellringer and also a singer. He helped to ring a peal in the Kenninghall Church bells of six-and-a-half hours duration, and composed a long piece of poetry about the feat.

"He was a very quaint and genial man. He was mostly called to the chair at our public meetings, and he used to tell us that when he was younger he had to work hard, live hard and lie hard. He was one of the labourers called to London to give evidence before the Royal Commission that was hearing evidence upon the franchise before the labourers obtained the vote."

The Franchise Bill was passed and became law in 1884. Labourers exercised the vote for the first time in the following year's General Election. Joseph Arch became their direct representative in the House of Commons when he won the North-West Norfolk seat by a majority of 640.

He was the first landworker to go to Parliament, and he kept ploughing straight furrows until he was 93. Someone wrote a poem in his honour (Kenninghall's George Edwards perhaps?), describing him as a "second Moses".

The last verse:
Surely 'tis right us Englishmen
And tillers of the land
That by our labour we should gain

What nature does demand.
I stand on the headlands watching man and nature drawing a timeless furrow or two. The gateway to winter is nudged open. The mists will turn to frosts, but we know logs are as cheery as sun or as star.

SQUIT ON INTERNET

It was a meeting made in cyberspace. She edged past animated huddles in the Great Saloon of Wolterton Hall and introduced herself as the woman who put squit on the internet.

Heads turned as the Traditional Trosher was forced to admit his role in employing trendy technology to spread the Norfolk message. Sighs of disbelief gave way to admiring glances as we exchanged cordial greetings.

Pauline Dodd, who moved from Yarmouth to Jersey with her architect husband in 1963, had returned to her native county just as Norfolk wit and squit clambered on to a stately-home podium.

My Press Gang troupe of local entertainers, scarcely used to stone cantilevered staircases, royal portraits and magnificent tapestries, were invited to Wolterton Hall by Lord and Lady Walpole in the name of homespun culture.

The sun was relishing a finale quadrille over the lake and parkland as we took a break for refreshments. Pauline forsook the pleasures of the balcony to report a growing global audience for the Norfolk dialect. She set up her web page a few months ago so surfers on the internet can turn on and tune in to the sound of Norfolk.

I offered to help when she wrote to me from the Channel Islands, although I made it quite clear that my renowned technological dyslexia would forestall any series of lectures on the international circuit.

I sent a book, cassette and excerpts with translations of the vernacular, and I gather my voice can be heard by anyone logging on to the Norfolk dialect page. "From Byways to Skyways and International Highways" ought to be the modest sales pitch – but I don't know how it all works.

Still, it is breathing new life into our dialect as the page is visited by grandchildren and great-grandchildren of Norfolk migrants who settled in the USA, Australia and all points on the compass across the globe. Squit in cyberspace must challenge Norfolk's image as the land that time ignored.

Marrying the old to the new like this is both a source of amusement and amazement to some. Pauline made a special journey home to remind us how it can be done, suitably enough in a building designed in the 1720s, abandoned in the middle of the last century, damaged by military occupation during the last war and a disastrous fire in 1952 and now being lovingly restored.

Pauline was accompanied by her father. He looked familiar, Yes, it was W R "Bob" Tuttle, clerk to the magistrates at Yarmouth when I was a young reporter in the town and carving my initials on the press benches in the Town Hall.

We chatted about the old days. Computers, surfers and web pages were pushed to one side for a few minutes. Pauline stood back and smiled an understanding smile.

SPORTING REUNION

After a gap of nearly 30 years, it was bound to seem a bit like a Norfolk version of Whatever Happened to the Likely Lads?

For Bob and Terry read Fish 'n' Arnie the double act from Beeston best remembered for staging three-week test matches and two-day soccer internationals to avoid an overdose of gainful employment during the summer holidays.

My 1950s nom-de-guerre was Freddie Fish, regularly filleted to the tail. One of my village playmates was Ernie Howe, known as the boy Arnie. He shared my passion for sport, cricket in particular, and our families, friends and foes always knew where to find us before bad light or fatigue stopped play.

Fish 'n' Arnie became Beeston shorthand for skiving, although we preferred to see our antics as healthy character-building. When we left the village to seek our fortunes, it was reported several older residents wept. It has been emphasised many times since that unmitigated joy can inspire tears.

Ernie joined the Army. I went to Thetford. Meetings faded into occasional phone calls. We lost touch. Then came the recent invitation to speak at a football club event in Lancashire. He just wanted to check if I could preach what I had been unable to practise on Lew Dack's meadow.

Ernie is commercial manager of Chorley FC, the Magpies of Victory Park, founded in 1883 and currently holding down a mid-table position in the Northern Premier League. The average gate is around 400, and their rivals include former League clubs Accrington Stanley and Barrow.

Our little reunion a few miles the other side of Manchester prompted minor bursts of rustic heckling. I told them Norfolk was nowhere near Dorset, and pointed out it was exactly 30 years since Norwich City's famous FA Cup victory at Old Trafford.

I made Don Heath and Gordon Bolland sound like household names.

Before the dinner, at which Ernie's fund-raising flair was as pronounced as the Northern accents all around us, I met the club directors, including former Burnley and England player Brian Pilkington.

One self-effacing sort of chap, who didn't want to sit at the top table, asked about parts of Norfolk and Suffolk where he had contacts in the holiday trade.

I asked Ernie about him. "Oh, he owns the club. He owns a fair bit of Lancashire, actually, and he's one of the richest men in the country. But there's absolutely no side to him. Same with everyone."

It's more pie-and-peas than caviar-and-champagne in the Northern Premier League. As I headed for home, Chorley travelled to Alfreton and scored a 3-0 victory. The supporters' bus broke down on the way there, and the Magpies had to wait until the second-half for proper backing.

"See you in 30 years!" called Ernie when I boarded the train at Chorley.

"Bring your bat and ball – and a drop of sunshine!" I called back as an icy wind nagged at the door.

The Fish 'n' Arnie Show is back in cold storage. Tickets for the 2027 revival on Lew Dack's meadow could be at a premium.

***

WITH BRUSSELS?
The spirit of European togetherness is alive and well in a farm gate in Norfolk: "For sale – new potatoes. (Twinned with pommes de terre)"

SQUIT WITH CHAIN GANG

It was too good an opportunity to pass up as the top brass of local government relaxed and waited for a blast from the parochial pulpit.

My invitation to speak at South Norfolk council's annual dinner at its pagoda-style headquarters in Long Stratton represented a considerable breakthrough for the Norfolk Home Guard.

Joining the cream of South Norfolk society were civic heads from all over Norfolk and Suffolk delighting in the collective name of "The Chain Gang" along with members of various organisations and the Armed Services. My host, South Norfolk chairman Tim East, nearing the end of his term of office, proposed a toast to the guests. I had to respond, but there were no instructions to be sycophantic, sensitive or even sceptical.

I was left entirely to my own desires and devices – the sort of opening afforded very few proud provincials in such exalted and cosmopolitan company.

Of course, good old-fashioned squit can build a useful bridge across shark-infested waters, and there must have been moments when complete harmony seemed likely to break out on the far shore.

But I pulled myself together in time, reminding our decision-makers that it was not politic to blame all difficulties on central government, however justified the ploy might seem. Nor could our elected representatives avoid image problems tied up in reputations for being rather aloof and cliquish.

With a glance towards an illustrious band of chief executives, I suggested that Norfolk's lack of a strong indigenous middle-class left the door open for incomers to dominate so many important local government posts.

No doubting their credentials, but an obvious risk of vital judgements being made without enough respect for or knowledge of Norfolk's past. Comparisons cannot hurt those who cannot make them.

Good mardling material there, and I was pleased to debate a few of the issues afterwards. It is always useful to seek solid ground between die-hards manning the drawbridge and missionaries preaching a gospel of progress and prosperity.

Alan Pask, chief executive of King's Lynn and West Norfolk council, pointed out there were exceptions to every rule. Born and raised at Earlham, he worked for South Norfolk council before taking up his present post. We agreed to differ over what might be good for our native county, especially when it came to housing developments.

Civilised discussion continued all the way home. I travelled with Bruce Barrell, chief executive of North Norfolk council.

My council tax bill had arrived in the morning. He didn't charge for the lift.

KING ARTHUR HOLDS COURT AT TRUNCH

Old friend and folk legend Sid Kipper warned against expecting too cordial a reception from the natives. He based all doubts on the experiences of his famous music-hall uncle, Jimmy "Am I Boring You?" Kipper, at the Trunch Empire.

Evidently, Jimmy kept his act on the brief side there simply because nobody stayed on stage long enough in the face of a notoriously hostile audience. "They used to reckon they left no turn unstoned" was Sid's moving salute to the good old days.

The sun has long set on the Trunch Empire and many other temples of Norfolk culture. But reputations linger, and so it was with some apprehension that I entered Trunch village to sing for my harvest supper, my first official engagement in a parish where they soon sort out whimsical wheat from churlish chaff.

I was seated next to a living legend, a man who puts even the redoubtable Sid Kipper in the shade when it comes to local knowledge and experience. Arthur Amis was born in Trunch in 1907 and he was soon regaling me with memories of life before and during the Great War.

He recalled this hall being built for just under £500 and then being taken over by the Army as their soldiers' cookhouse and dining area. At a concert where locals were allowed to join in , a soldier gave an exhibition of step-dancing.

Next day, Frank Clark, the head team-man, said of the soldier's stirring performance "My word, he could handle his feet!"

So that was the ploy, to undermine any plans to tell yarns with whiskers on by confronting me early with a sage of the soil who has ploughed just about every humorous furrow this century.

It might have been a chastening experience, but the twinkling Arthur, who could milk a cow when he was three, assured me there was no skulduggery afoot. I heard they had named a road after him in the village, a rare honour to be bestowed on someone still about to appreciate it.

"Yes – and two of the people who live in Amis Close are sitting opposite us." What a glorious icebreaker! I mardled with the newcomers from Buckinghamshire, who said they were learning so much about Norfolk in general and Trunch in particular from a copy of Arthur's memoirs, From Dawn to Dusk, first published four years ago.

After a splendid supper built around hot potatoes, the company felt benign enough to leave the turn unstoned, or even pebble-dashed. Arthur was so sorry to miss any gems floating down toward the cleared tables, but the batteries had gone suddenly in his hearing aid. "I tried to smile in the right places by watching all the others," he confided.

Another stalwart of the Norfolk agricultural scene came striding over the headlands as I made for Swaffham Festival to present a selection of extracts from my favourite local authors. Former farmworker's leader Jack Boddy was in puckish mood.

He told how a grey squirrel was causing havoc in his walnut tree, and one or two drawn into his interval coterie prolonged the fun by cheering for the squirrel. It was that sort of evening, full of homely leg-pulling among old friends.

Of course, Arthur Amis and Jack Boddy would have proved ideal companions on my latest visit to Norfolk Rural Life Museum at Gressenhall. Not that I was disappointed with colleagues on the local entertainment scene raising their voices in the refurbished workhouse chapel.

The chief fund-raising drive at Gressenhall this year has been to make the old chapel suitable for all sorts of events, nights of Norfolk culture included.

The slope of the floor takes some getting used to and the place can be on the chilly side for performers and spectators alike. Even so, good acoustics and true character suggest this could be a valuable centre if money and time continue to be spent wisely.

Those with long memories say it has much more potential than was ever realised during the most successful years of the old Trunch Empire when Jimmy "Am I Boring You?" Kipper turned survival into an art form.

LITTLE TROSHING HAS TIME ON HANDS

Little Troshing (also incorporating the decayed parishes of Barleysele and Bindertwine) has decided to set the rest of Norfolk a stirring example by going ahead with its own Great Millennium Project.

This remote hamlet of 56 souls, all but 37 of them wholly committed to an exercise described as "the sticking plaster of bold ambition designed to heal petty divisions and bring us closer together", is taking the solo path after an emotional gathering in the Old Rectory orchard.

Miss Harper, in the chair for an inaugural meeting of the New Little Troshing Millennium Ideas Forum, said they had to play safe because there was every chance they were the privileged successors to an Old Little Troshing Millennium Ideas Forum. The fact they had not yet come across any minutes to this effect should not prohibit respect for proper committee procedures.

Parish council chairman, retired dentist Amos Horkey, broadly agreed, although he was reasonably happy to accept the word of oldest resident Granny Pinkerton when she told him only that morning she had thought long and hard but could not call to mind such an organisation being set up before in the village.

"She does remind us that the old Norfolk word for pumpkin is million and a lot of people used to be for 'em..." Miss Harper, lips pursed, glasses perched on the bridge of her noble nose and steel-grey eyes flashing, dared him to continue. Amos Horkey mumbled to a halt. "...but I really don't think that ought to cause any confusion."

Miss Harper called for suggestions from the floor or, as she amended it when none were forthcoming, brainwaves from the grass. The evening air was soporific, but Billy Windham was keen to enhance his burgeoning reputation as a one-man think tank. His years as a traffic warden in Chelmsford had given him access to fruitful avenues so often closed to others.

"Why don't we save up our funds and bright ideas and put them all towards a really big do to mark the year 2000?" He was impressed by his own shrewdness and treated hoots of derision as nothing more than blatant envy. They'd thank him as soon as it became clear they were way ahead of countless bigger communities in marking a major milestone.

Retired bank manager Ernest Dough-Jones said he knew a man in the City who knew the lady whose sister-in-law cleaned for Virginia Bottomley, and it might be worth a note to the Millennium Commission to tell them they could count on useful support from the private sector if Little Troshing's application for funds was given favourable consideration.

As no one quite understood what that meant, Percy Smuckerling, retired advertising consultant, said he was going to run this one up the flagpole and see who was likely to salute. "Why don't we swallow our pride a little and join forces with our smaller neighbours to make it a district project?"

Miss Harper's steel-grey eyes flashed again. There could be no doubting her anger as she looked straight at Percy Smuckerling and addressed the entire gathering.

"It is common knowledge that Lower Dodman, Upper Muckwash and Puckaterry Parva all refused to take any part whatsoever in the Coronation Pageant of June 1911, an act of unprecedented selfishness compounded by a similar rebuff when we requested assistance with our Silver Jubilee celebrations in May, 1935. There have been no apologies, either verbal or written, and so our non-cooperation policy remains firmly intact. Subject closed!"

So, only schemes conceived in Little Troshing, designed solely for the benefit of inhabitants of the parish and financed entirely by them. Ernest Dough-Jones presumed there was no point in trying to contact Virginia Bottomley or her cleaning lady.

Two hours later, as the light faded, the millennium shortlist was ready despite Billy Windham's announcement that he still felt they ought to channel all this enthusiasm into a really big do to greet the year 2000.

A replacement bus shelter was rejected because there was no bus service in the village – hadn't been for 34 years – and it would only encourage late-night unpleasantness on the part of the Lower Dodman Over-60s Motorcycle and Sidecar Club.

A statue of Little Troshing's most notable personality to be erected in front of the Old Bakery was turned down when Miss Harper intimated she was very flattered but had no intention of dying before the end of the century.

New pews for the church were vetoed as it was pointed out that the average congregation numbered four, a significant 13 fewer than the number of parishes under the pastoral umbrella of the Rev. Septimus "Happyclappy" Clayton.

A village sign on the green had to be ruled out of the question as no one could recall where the green was before development, and there were bound to be fierce arguments over subjects to be featured on the sign.

The only "famous" character in Little Troshing history was Nathaniel Porterhouse, a 19th century squire and opium addict who ravished all maidens within a 15-mile radius. Legend had it he fell off his horse and perished when he tried to abduct two buxom serving wenches outside the manor house in Puckaterry Parva.

That left a new clock to be installed above the portrait of King George V in the Reading Room. Miss Harper was thrilled when the idea was greeted with unanimous approval. Her steel-grey eyes lit up with the eagerness of a Scarlett O'Hara surrounded by admirers anxious to dance to her music.

"A very wise choice if I may say so on both practical and aesthetic grounds!

"And there can be only one name for the Little Troshing Millennium Project to remind us how the old clock on the wall can be the only winner in our eternal battle against time..."

She ignored a rheumatic twinge. The vote was a formality. They loved the sound of Ticknopolis.

***

TALE OF TWO TEETH
Younger son extracted a remarkable double out of a family trip over the border. He began the car journey with two wobbly bottom teeth and a clear desire to catch up with some of his gap-happy classmates.
The first tooth yielded to delicate wiggling while we were still in Norfolk. The second gave way a matter of minutes into Suffolk We were delighted not to be heading for Scotland.
His two-county antics came as a severe blow to the family reputation for parochialism and inspired painful puns about rooting for Mr. Gummer's constituency.
Charity begins at home, of course, and the tooth fairy was waiting in the wings at Cromer. Probably becorth it can't thay Thuffolk properly.
The wife and I completed an intriguing weekend double of our own. We attended the annual dinner of Bradenham Cricket Club in the village where Henry Rider Haggard was born in 1856.
The following day's outing took us through Ditchingham, where he was buried in 1925.

GRAVE MISTAKE

Intriguing tailpiece from Bressingham, near Diss, where the village pub, The Garden House, is directly opposite the church.

A couple were enjoying a meal recently at the pub as evening light faded. Suddenly, the woman, sitting near a window through which you can see the churchyard, turned rather white and dropped her knife and fork.

"One of those tombstones just moved!" she cried. "Trick of the light, get on with your dinner." retorted her partner.

A few minutes later she dropped her cutlery again and insisted one of the tombstones had definitely moved, This time the man pushed his chair round so he could clearly see the churchyard as well.

Sure enough, he saw the same thing. They called for the bill and fully intended to leave without finishing their meal. The landlord asked what was wrong. They told him what they had seen – what they had both seen through the window.

He laughed a hearty landlord laugh. There were a couple of sheep in the churchyard to keep the grass short. In the twilight their colour was indistinguishable from the tombstones!

So, if you go to Bressingham don't make the same grave mistake. Don't accuse your partner of trying to pull the wool over your eyes. Of course, you could always play safe and order a baa meal... they won't fleece you.

***

SLOW BUSINESS
A Norfolk newspaper reporter was told of a village where there hadn't been a funeral for over 20 years. "They seemed to live there forever!" he scribbled in his notebook.
He decided to investigate. On reaching the village he was shocked to see a funeral procession about to enter the church. He turned to a bystander and exclaimed: "They told me nobody ever died in this parish. Here I am on my first visit, and what do I see but a funeral! Who is the unlucky parishioner? What did he die of?"
The ancient local stroked his chin and answered quietly: "Oh, that ent no parishner. Thass the doctor. Jist died o' starvearshun."

PROFESSOR OF DIALECT

What is the connection between squit and sociolinguistics? Or the Boy John Letters and an academic conference in Finland?

Professor Peter Trudgill provided the answers on taking a break from his Swiss base at the University of Lausanne. He is an international expert in the dialect field – and proud of his Norfolk roots.

On one of his frequent returns to home soil, we enjoyed a lengthy mardle about our sense of humour, the language that goes with it and the chances of their survival.

Born in Norwich, with all his 16 great-great-grandparents coming from the east of the county, he attended the City of Norwich School and studied modern languages at King's College, Cambridge. Now Professor of English Linguistics at the University of Lausanne, his work on the close link between language and society is seen as a key weapon in the fight against a culturally standardised world.

He showed me a paper he presented to a Helsinki conference last year. The title hardly rolled off the tongue – Dedialectalisation and Norfolk Dialect Orthography – but I soon warmed to its contents.

Starting point was the controversy in the EDP letters columns during the summer of 1996 over the correct spelling of "beautiful" in the Norfolk dialect. I lined up with the "bewtiful" brigade against the "bootiful" voters, and it was a delight to find Professor Trudgill coming out in favour of the former.

He also examined dialect literature, with particular reference to the Boy John Letters sent by Sidney Grapes to the EDP between 1946 and 1958, "work of not a little genius".

Professor Trudgill told his audience: "Not only were the characterisations and vignettes of village life brilliant, and therefore enormously popular, but Sidney Grapes was also a superb writer of the local dialect, right down to subtleties such as Granfar speaking in a more conservative, traditional way than the other characters."

While humour is a key component in Norfolk's fight to do different, the Professor warns that if dialects are to survive they must be used in as wide a range of contexts as possible.

"The Norfolk dialect is a vital means of helping preserve Norfolk values, culture, way of life. It is also important, more than many other dialects, since it is one of the last dialects in the

South of England, and especially the South-East of England, to remain relatively distinctive and relatively widely spoken."

Will it survive? "Yes, though, like all dialects, it will continue to change. It is most likely to survive if we can engender and preserve positive attitudes to all forms of Norfolk English – that is, not just traditional country speech but also the traditional and more recent vernaculars of Norwich and Yarmouth."

Can our schools do more? "Yes, by fostering pride and interest, and by countering snobbery and negative feelings. Teachers should be able to say what the main points of the grammar, vocabulary and pronunciation of the dialect are. And they should be able to encourage dialect in some form of written work, not just humorous forms."

Professor Trudgill soon completed his homework, My Favourite Dialect Story. It comes from H V Morton's In Search of England:

"I was lost in a Norfolk lane, so I stopped a man and I said to him: 'Good morning!' He looked at me. 'Good morning!' I cried. 'Can you tell me if I am right for Norwich?'

"He continued to look at me. Then, in an uneasy, suspicious way, he said: 'What d'ye want to know for?'"

***

THEY DEW SAY
Tom: How dew yew know yew're tew old ter play cricket?
Horry: Blarst, I hed that one sorted owt years ago.
Tom: What, when yer legs started slowin' up an yew coont git yer wind?
Horry: No, bor, when th'umpyres started ter look young!

***

PARKING LOT
A couple of visitors from Kent thought they had hit on a foolproof way of finding their way back to the car after going for a meal in Norwich. "Now, just remember we've parked outside a medieval church..."
A three-hour search told them to head for the cathedral next time.

TAKING DICKEY OUT OF OLD CUSTOMS

When I was a lad, anniversaries meant a packed chapel, a visiting preacher with a dinner-plate button-hole, recitations on crumpled paper behind your back in case of emergency and a handsome collection towards the annual seaside outing.

We had the odd Coronation street party, Jubilee tea and thanksgiving supper to mark the end of a war or the start of a new blackberry-picking campaign.

Generally, though, we sauntered along as willing hostages to the rolling seasons, calling "holdgee!" at harvest time, "hold hard!" at closing time and wondering why we couldn't find the white snowplough when winter winds blew and cut us off from the rest of the world.

We had to make our own amusements – hence a penchant for white snowploughs, loosely-tethered goats on the green, inkwells full of frogspawn, collapsible bicycle seats, swivelling signposts to confuse the Vikings and a smoking Tortoise stove in the chapel to shorten the sermons.

It was harmless rural fun to complement the regular rhythms of a Norfolk largely at ease with itself. Communities were small and closely-knit, tied to the land and the eternal secrets of overgrown headlands and bountiful hedgerows. There was also genuine satisfaction in knowing where the fun came from. No question of the wrong person finishing up in the stocks or in the barrel of rotten apples behind the pub.

Times change. Country life has lost much of its spontaneity while demands for it to be revived are on the increase. New villagers, often drawn by ancient tales of rustic rituals designed to keep indigenous folk amused before satellite dishes, orienteering and real ale, are digging up anniversaries by the barrow-load.

Happenings that used to occur so easily no one thought them unusual, or even peculiar to a particular area, now assume a mystique bordering on the supernatural.

Take the traditional Norfolk routine of dickey-dawdling, where rival hamlets reflected the virtues of a gentler, more reflective age by pitting their slowest donkeys against each other on the last Saturday in July.

The animal taking longest to complete the two-furlong course on neutral territory, while deemed not to have stopped or taken on board any form of sustenance at any stage of the journey, was crowned King Dickey in the first week of August – if the competition had ended.

There are moves to revive this rural delight in the west of the county, but using traffic wardens on old-fashioned bicycles instead of perambulating donkeys. Arts Council backing is promised, but purists say it simply won't be the same. They have a point.

We have seen the socially significant and deeply moving Soak the Suffragette manifestation of Edwardian country-house gatherings reduced to a garden fete knockabout side-show called Drench the Wench. So politically incorrect it mocks all progress made in certain departments this century.

We have heard the brave new custodians of revels, festivals and wakes confuse swan-upping at Downham with pint-downing at Upton. We have winced at the questioning of fertility-inducing merits of rolling pork cheeses along disused railway lines (the pre-Beeching era was remarkable for its lack of complaints about the habit.)

We know there is reluctance to accept the Dunmow Flitch as a Norfolk custom in origin, despite firm evidence it was popular in the 13th century as the Dunhame Itche. Married couples resident in either Grete or Littel Dunhame who could prove they had not uttered a civil word to each other during a period of at least seven years and a day after the wedding were given leave to separate, along with a voucher for a side of salted beef.

It all adds up to serious doubts about the amount of due care and attention likely to be paid by those claiming to seek country anchors in a changing world. From well-undressing for hardy maidens on January 15 to forelock-tugging for those of a subservient disposition on any five dates in October, well-loved Norfolk ceremonies and customs must be retained as comfortingly fixed points on the calendar.

Tomorrow, of course, is Dogrose Day when courting couples all over the county will be up early to catch the morning on those lovely hedgerow flowers for the traditional cheek-brushing rites.

The beau chants this refrain as his dew-damp fingers caress his loved one's face:

Ask not the reason from whence it did spring
For you know very well 'tis an old ancient thing.

A ritual unrivalled in its summer simplicity and beauty. But if you want to anticipate a real winter warmer, which still perplexes multitudes of Norfolk newcomers, I recommend a practice set strong in pagan soil.

A dank November day, with rain, fog, frost or mud round the edges, is an ideal setting for Beeting the Raretreat. To renew your vows to Mother Earth, you must wear a tattered cap, collarless shirt, open waistcoat, overalls with sacking tied to the knees, hobnailed boots without laces and a smile that looks genuine.

Select two items from a large root crop, one in either hand, and bang them together to banish dark underground forces. Place them neatly in line for your following companion (male or female) to defoliate with one swish of a sharp hook to signify the frailty of Mother Earth's children. At the end of each row, after a swig of cold tea, both participants bow, turn and prepare for more action with the incantation:

Come, guard the bounty, for us there's no stoppin'
It's bewtiful weather for knockin' and toppin'
Norfolk can ill afford to surrender such fertile ground.

***

TASTY MEMORIES
Winnie Chapman was a character and a cook of the old school.
My old grammar school at Swaffham, in fact, and she served up delicious helpings of memories as we shared several reunions in recent years.
She died just short of her 86th birthday after a long and happy retirement close to her loving family at Sporle.
Winnie could match all my yarns from Hamond's when she reflected on her dinner lady days before, during and after my Swaffham career.
She recalled keeping watch for boys who dared to go out of the school gate minus a cap, darning holes in the seats of their trousers after rough-and-tumble escapades, finding them a few coppers out of her own purse to spend at the tuck shop – and even chasing one of the masters with a dishcloth before discovering his true identity!
"I thought he was one of the boys, and he took it all in good part," she smiled.
That was Winnie's strength. She could always muster an extra helping of compassion when needed to go with the spotted dick and custard.

FINDING THE WAY

Jonathan Mardle, whose talents illuminated the EDP for many years, was quick to emphasise the difference between Broad Norfolk and Broad Norwich.

He claimed the latter had at its worst degenerated into an adenoidal gabble, and told a famous story to prove the point:

"A stranger came up to me in Norwich's London Street and asked the way to 'Largo Lane'. I was puzzled, and was about to say I had never heard of it, when suddenly the light dawned, and I realised that the stranger had been directed in Broad Norwich to Lower Goat Lane, which the Norwich tongue would have distorted into 'La'r Goo' Lay'."

That yarn came back to me while I was reading a fascinating book about Kirby Bedon, three miles south-east of Norwich, penned in 1924 by the rector of the parish, the Rev E H Kinder. He told a similar story:

"A stranger arrived at Thorpe Station, where he asked the way to a street on the other side of the city. He was told he must go to Luke Spells and was given directions.

"He was puzzled at being directed to a man instead of a place. As he went along the unfamiliar streets, from time to time he asked his way to Luke Spells. Directions were promptly given; everyone seemed to know him.

"He arrived at the lower part of Exchange Street – Post Office Street at that time – and asked a small child the way to Luke Spells. To his surprise even the child knew him, and told him to turn at the end of the street and he would be nearly there. Once more he asked for Luke Spells. The answer was: 'There – right opposite.'

"It was Duke's Palace. Following the vernacular fairly well, he had been asking for Duke's Palace, i.e. Dook's Pels, as Luke Spells – and he found it!"

***

THEY DEW SAY
Horry: Dew yew wurry bowt gittin' olde?
Tom: Nut eny more....cors that dew hev its consolearshuns ...
Horry: Like whot?
Tom: Well, for a start yew kin whistle while yew brush yar teeth!

PAST AND FUTURE UNITE

Recent rural rides, beautifully trimmed with primrosed banks and trumpeting daffodils, took me well beyond cosy nostalgic corners.

Fond memories were roused. It is impossible to visit certain places on my Norfolk circuit without holding hands with the past. But I caught glimpses of a bright and bold future as well. Village schools and halls dominated my March outings list, as I met people pursuing specific targets with relish and unashamed good humour.

The James Bradfield Community Primary School at Stoke Ferry has "founding the future" as its motto.

Our Press Gang concert party may have dipped freely into yesterday's inkwell for some material, but over £250 was raised for the school's computers and technology area. Ancient and modern combining effectively.

North Elmham Memorial Hall provided a solo stage. I arranged a Norfolk Bouquet for the local flower festival committee – readings and reflections tied up with a bit of squit.

Nearly £200 blossomed forth towards the cost of running the flower festival at St Mary's over the August bank holiday weekend.

Bradenham Village Hall, nestling by the green, was packed out to greet Press Gang ranks, and we were treated to baked potatoes and the trimmings before being invited to justify a menu crammed with old chestnuts. Still, they were tasty enough to help raise over £400 towards a local play area.

Carleton Rode Village Hall was next stop for our entertainment wagon. Locals here are busy learning the ropes to mark the new millennium in style, swelling funds to reinstall a peal of six bells at the parish church.

The spire at All Saints' collapsed in the 1750s and the poor villagers had to sell five of the bells to pay for church repairs. the drive to put matters right some 250 years on is gathering pace, aided by a handsome donation from USAF veterans who have village links from the last war.

Great Dunham Primary School, standing proudly next door to the parish church, offers one of Norfolk's most telling answers to those who still insist the writing's on the wall for these small seats of learning in the country.

A glowing reputation has been enhanced by an £80,000

extension, incorporating a new library and long-awaited inside lavatories.

After my school dinner – "What, Monday without stew, cabbage or lumpy custard?" – and a series of classroom mardles with pupils, teachers, governors and the drop-in brigade, I cut the ribbon to a new era.

Naturally, I was tempted into yarns from my days at Beeston School a few miles up the road, where they're still waiting for the end of outside toilets.

Thankfully, the young Dunham welcoming committee hauled me back with a splendid anthology of their poems dealing with pressing matters of today.

Here's a small sample of one-liners to inspire us on our April rounds.

Boredom is sitting in the car when Mum is talking.

Embarrassment is a photo of you naked with chicken-pox.

Happiness is getting to school on time.

Humour is the dog cocking his leg up on your enemy's car.

***

VEGETABLE PLOT
Billy was in prison for something he didn't do – he didn't wear gloves. He knew all the prison mail was censored.
He got a letter from his wife asking about the family garden: "When dew I plant the spuds?"
He wrote back: "Dunt yew dig up our garden. Thass where I buried all that money."
His wife wrote back a few days later: "Six policemen came ter the house, an' they dug up every square inch o' the back garden."
By return of post she got the answer: "Right – now yew kin plant the spuds!"

***

THEY DEW SAY
Horry: Hev yew sin the docter bowt yar knee trubble?
Tom: Yeh, an' he say the pain in m' ryte knee is down ter owld age.
Horry: Blarst, that carn't be ryte...
Tom: No, both m' knees are searme age – an' thuther wun's okay!

GOLDEN DAY RUINED BY WRECKED SEAT

I should have been basking in the bronze glow of autumn and totting up reasons for voting September my favourite month.

Suddenly, dog mess became more obvious than dahlias, litter upstaged turning leaves and familiar regrets blew in.

"Have you seen what they've done?" asked a man carrying two bags of shopping and the unmistakable air of an old soldier enraged and perplexed by signs of modern conflict at the top of the loke.

A wooden seat, presented in memory of a grateful resident 20 years ago, had been butchered by sharp instruments and dull minds, its back broken, gouged out and smashed into a funeral pyre beneath the sad remnants.

A morning full of sunshine, birdsong and cheery greetings was reduced to a bitter commentary on the disease of destruction.

"It's the same everywhere," was the predictable epitaph for a wrecked seat, a helpless, hopeless statement to go with the kindling of chaos waiting to be ignited below.

This sense of impotence followed me for the rest of a day I had intended to elevate to September's roll of honour.

Instead of counting blessings I railed against everything in general and no one in particular for allowing vandalism, dirt, noise and intolerance to become just part of our bustling lives.

I tried hard to convince myself that this could be dismissed as another melodramatic, self-righteous torrent of indignation from someone lucky enough to be shown right from wrong in an era when demarcation lines were heavily drawn.

Other places in Norfolk have worse problems than Cromer, but it was natural to feel more anger, fear and frustration when they surfaced so close to home.

And that's where we have to look for reasons and solutions – close to home.

No chance of an end-of-season reverie while this mood persisted. Roaring traffic seemed to trumpet defiance as I attempted to cross the road.

The paths to Cromer Pier, with its reviving powers built on fresh air and tradition, were paved with bad inventions, most of them plastic, crumpled and hurled down within sight of a litter bin.

"The nights are pulling in," announced a woman making short work of an ice-cream.

Normally, the observation would inspire warm, cosy images of curtains drawn and tea beside the fire.

Not today, you seat-wreckers. Today it was an ominous warning of wanton destruction carried out under the cowardly cloak of darkness.

We have been told that our concerns are exaggerated, that fear of crime has raced ahead of crime itself. There's a lot of clever talk about misconceptions, and we are bound to get extra rations as the political parties assemble for their last table-thumping, foot-stomping, flag-waving conferences before the general election.

Anti-social behaviour in all its grubby guises has bitten deep into the fabric of Norfolk life in recent years, in city, town and village.

The fact that "it's the same everywhere" cannot hide a fundamental need to seek local answers to local problems.

If we simply leave them to police and politicians, some distance away from cause and effect, we break the first rule of any self-respecting community – to care for itself.

If that means pointing the finger at those who show blatant disregard for any rules, well, let the pointing start in earnest.

A wrecked wooden seat in Cromer does not rank as the darkest symbol of decadence and decline, real or perceived. But it ruined a golden September day I wanted to store away, and it posed an awkward question many would prefer to ignore.

Is it that long ago when such an act of vandalism would have prompted an outcry in a seaside resort proud to be known as the Gem of the Norfolk Coast?

***

PANCAKE FACTOR
I strolled carefully over a brownfield site the other evening.
It was a greenfield site not long ago, but cattle have a way of leaving their distinctive mark on the countryside.
They do it mainly to confuse inexperienced government housing and environment folk who threaten to follow the old herd instinct when it comes to locations for thousands of new houses. The Pancake Factor could yet play a part in saving Norfolk from turning into Essex
A pat on the back, please, for guardians of the pastures.

COUNTRYSIDE CUSTODIANS

When I was a lad, and much closer to the Norfolk soil than I am now, it was easy to be in awe of farmers.

They owned all that land and property. They provided work for many people in the locality, numbers rising dramatically for the sugar beet and corn harvests.

Yes, there was a whiff of feudalism lingering over our rural scene, especially where families lived in tied cottages which went with the jobs. Wages were poor alongside those on offer in town and city.

But farmers who treated their acres and workers with genuine respect brought a sense of security to a pastoral picture destined to change beyond recall within a couple of decades.

It may be too simple to cite mechanisation and the Common Agricultural Policy as main reasons for the revolution, but we know button-pushing and form-filling now take precedence over muck-spreading and crop-tilling.

Farmers are on the march to draw attention to an industry struggling to keep its head above the headlands. Leaving aside any details of what happened when angry employees tried that one themselves in the name of family survival, most notably in the 1920s, I admit my awe has turned to sympathy.

Falling farm incomes must affect the rural economy as a whole. Only one brick in the wall, I know, but a continuing decline in fortunes will encourage the surrender of many more precious green acres for house-building. Developers are rubbing their hands in anticipation.

Diversification of recent years, golf courses, farm shops and holiday cottages leading the way, told us the old order had gone. But that did not prepare us for the possibility of a countryside without a soul at the end of this century.

At the heart of this dilemma are farmers, many of them ploughing an old family furrow, who know it is only a matter of time before they have to leave the land.

To whom? More executive dwellers who want to play pretend gentry? Fresh hordes of trippers seeking respite from the rigours and stresses of urban life? Grasping builders backed by a government which denounced a frightening development tide when in oppositions and now seems to have changed its mind?

Whatever we think of the present generation of "custodians of the countryside", I fear the next will be mighty short on compassion, commitment and conservation. Agri-business and concrete mixers have no truck with such niceties.

For all the deep-rooted problems, and threats of more to come, Arcadian longings will continue to add peculiar pressures of their own. A rural fantasy, fed by Whitehall mandarins and Westminster politicians confronted with unreasonable demands for new homes in the country, simply remains too useful to put to flight.

Making a fetish out of the rural and the rustic whets appetites and sells houses. Fewer experienced and successful farmers to counter such arrant nonsense leaves another gate open to the voracious field-eaters.

***

IN SHORT.....
The new village parson asked old George the best way to keep his congregation interested.
"Well, ole partner, we allus rekun the secret of a good sarmun is a good berginnin' and a good endin'," said George.
The parson smiled his gratitude. But George hadn't finished. "And leavin' em as close tergether as possible!"

***

POTATO RINGS
A Norfolk farmer asked one of his workers to go to the telephone box in the village and ring up the Potato Marketing Board.
About an hour later the farmer went to the phone box and found his man still inside. He asked if he had made the call.
"Cor, blarst, give a bloke a charnse," came the reply. "I hev bin a'lookin' threw the Ts fer Taters... but I'm beggared if I kin find it ennywhere."

***

THEY DEW SAY
Tom: Whot dew yew call a man who give in when he's wrong, old partner?
Horry: Rekun he's smart...
Tom: An' what dew yew call a man who give in when he myte be ryte?
Horry: Rekun he's married!

LITTLE TROSHING'S COVER-UP PLAN

Little Troshing (also incorporating the decayed parishes of Barleysele and Bindertwine) has given its verdict.

This Norfolk hamlet of 56 souls – some of them irretrievably lost according to the man who delivers paraffin every other Wednesday – wants no truck with campaigns to attract more tourists to quiet areas.

A packed public meeting in the scullery of Dunyankin, home of retired dentist and parish council chairman Amos Horkey, voted unanimously to write to the Rural Development Commission expressing "serious disquiet" over a recent survey suggesting tourism could play an important role in strengthening the social and economic life of countryside communities.

"We should continue to implement the twin-track approach which has served this precious pocket of old England so admirably since the war" said Miss Harper from the Old Rectory. Lack of applause, or even a nod of approval, told her to explain.

"If they find the way in, we show them the way out!" Loud cheers and a break for warmed-up sausage rolls and piping hot cocoa to celebrate.

Miss Harper said she was referring to the Boer War.

During the interval retired bank manager Ernest Dough-Jones arrived late to draw passionate requests not to deliver another boring lecture on the single currency, a stakeholder economy or the virtue of Technopolis.

"Let's cover up all the signposts within a five-mile radius and tell the county council we didn't know the war was over if they notice!" he enthused as the meeting resumed. That was hardly fair on the neighbouring parishes of Lower Dodman, Upper Muckwash and Puckaterry Parva, said Mr Horkey, but it remained a tactic well worth considering if the roads became extra busy by Easter.

Mr Dough-Jones said he was referring to the first world war.

Billy Windham, always ready to see the other point of view after a long and successful career as a traffic warden in Chelmsford, said they had to move with the times.

"Yes, tourism can have a backside..."

"Downside" interrupted Miss Harper. Then she put a smile in her voice and added quietly, "Come to think of it, William, your description is more apt."

He continued as if nothing else had been said... "but look what it could do for the pub, the shop, the museum, the garden centre, the art gallery, the takeaway, the laundrette, the garage and the cafe!"

A perplexed chairman spoke for the rest. "But we don't have any of those things in Little Troshing, as you well know..."

"Ah, but we COULD have them all and many more priceless amenities if we were on the tourism trail. You can get grants, and we being in an area of outstanding natural beauty... OUCH!"

A cooled-down sausage roll caught him flush on the forehead. Thankfully the pastry was flaky and light and so damage was confined to a few bruises in Billy's pride. He laughed uneasily as retired advertising consultant Percy Smuckerling said the thought of Billy wearing his uniform again was enough to inspire a call for a total ban on traffic in the parish.

After that the democratic process ran its course. Mr Horkey called for a unanimous vote against any kind of rural exploitation, and reminded the gathering that next week's meeting of the Well-Dressing Club in the front room had been cancelled because of the outing.

"The charabanc leaves from outside the old bakery at 9.30am sharp. Don't forget your maps, camera, suntan lotion, floppy hats, packed lunches, guide books and travel sickness pills.

"Who knows, there might be time to ask a few locals if Wroxham really needs a bypass before we head for the wildlife park. Better bring your wellingtons, Miss Harper..."

Mr Smuckerling made a weak joke about Lancasters not being needed as the good folk of Little Troshing bade their farewells and filed out to marvel at a still and starlit Norfolk night.

Mr Smuckerling said he was referring to the second world war.

***

PLENTY OF TIME
Back in the days of the sporting parsons in Norfolk, two labourers were muck-spreading and watching a hunt in the distance.
One said to the other: "Blarst, there's a rider orf his hoss a'layin' in the ditch."
"So there is," said the other. "Blowed if that ent th'ole rector."
The first labourer simply leaned on his muck fork.
"Let him stay there," he said. "He wunt be wanted agin till next Sunday."

NORFOLK SALUTE TO ST. GEORGE

Now St George he dint sit abowt yappin'
Or polishin' his hearlow orl day,
No, he git them good folk a'clappin'
By keepin' rottin beggars at bay.
"If thass a rare sortin-owt they're arter,
They kin he' wun wi'owt enny dowt,
Jist a ding o'the lug for a starter
...An' then a good poke o' the snowt!"
Wun nyte he wuz hevin' a sharbert
Wi' the boys down the ole Cherry Tree,
When orl of a suddin' Boy Harbert
Fell ter the floor – on wun knee.
"Woss up wi' yew?" say Billa Stratton,
Boy Harbert, he coont say a lot,
So he mearke 'em orl garp at the cattan...
An' then he dermand a fresh pot.
The fearce at the winder wuz grimy –
No wunder young Harbert wuz sceared –
An' then green scales orl twisted an' slimy,
Sorter cuverin' a straggly grey beard.
St George he drink up his sweet sherry
An' put his nuts back in the packit,
An' then he trearpse orf sorter merry
While the rest onnem kick up a rackit.
He cum back bowt ten minnits arter,
His shat wuz orl tattered an' torn,
His trowsers, they wunt much smarter,
My hart, he did look forlorn.
"Thass the wyfe wi' a little reyminder
That I hent dun the hoovrin terday,
She gi' me a rare Swardeston Wynder,
When will that all end now, I pray?"
Poor George, he order a gret flaggun
O' the strongest beer 'hind the bar.
"I'm orff ter fyte anuther draggun
- But wi' this wun yew know where yew are!
I kin stick fyre an' smook an' sum sinjin,
Yis, thass orl part o' the gearme –
But when my ole gal start a'winjin'
Wuh, I crumble and curl up in shearme."

So, there yew are my ole bewties,
Fore yew hoss ter the pub fit ter bust,
Jist yew 'member them tyme-honoured dewties...
An' dew the bludder hooverin' fust!

Keith Skipper, 1993

BOOK ENDS

Church towers dominate the Norfolk countryside. From any point of vantage, the gentle unemphatic landscape of farmland and woodland rolls away, mile after mile, to the dim horizon of the sea. Slowly and subtly the colours change with the seasons and the crops: corn and roots, stubble and ploughland, olland and pasture, gorse and bracken, the beechwoods and the ash-carrs and the oaks in the hedgerows, all contribute to build up a scene which unceasingly alters as the months go by.

Unchanged against this ever-varying background of colour stand the grey flint towers rising in every village above cottage roofs or from groups of ancient trees. Each tower represents many centuries of history; it stood there before the cottages and the trees, and it will outlast them, an emblem of the continuity of English life.

R W Ketton-Cremer, A Norfolk Gallery, 1948

***

The country is all eyes and ears. You are alone, walking through a wood maybe or down a narrow footpath between high hedges: you can't be seen. But the chap hoeing three fields away will hear the panicky treble clap of the pigeon clattering out of an ivied tree or the alarm call of a blackbird, see a rook or jackdaw pull up in passage and circle twice, high above where you are moving. Automatically he will mark your invisible progress, until he is satisfied who you are and what you are up to.

It is one of the saddest things about the modern countryman that he no longer uses his eyes and ears, or indeed any other of his senses, in this way; he is relatively oblivious to what is going on around him and unaware of what he is missing. And, alas, this oblivion extends to his work, too. The tractor driver goes on, regardless of what he may be doing to the land, where the oldster behind his team not only saw and heard what his implement was doing but felt through the soles of his boots what was happening inches below the harrow teeth or drill coulter.

Hugh Barrett, Early to Rise, 1967

***

Norfolk villages convey, if not a sense of the picturesque, a beauty born of a thousand years of life, a millennium of man's eternal struggle.

It is a far more deeply felt beauty than the superficial. It changes much across the fourth largest county of England. Below South Lopham where the River Waveney almost meets the River Little Ouse, and a single thin sliver of road joins Norfolk to the rest of England, there is the same feeling of independence as there is on Mundesley beach.

To watch the sun set in the sea at Dersingham or Snettisham and rise again at Sea Palling or Caister is to experience a feeling that this independence matters.

David Kennett, Norfolk Villages, 1980

***

I have just returned from a weekend in Norfolk. From the conversation at the dinner table on the first evening I gathered that my great crime against Norfolk is that I, a mere Southerner, have dared to criticise this county in any way whatsoever. Apparently Norfolk is beyond criticism...

Norfolk is a farming county. There one talks farming, thinks farming, dreams farming, and lives farming almost to the exclusion of all else; but the only farming which is considered worthy of notice is the type of farming which has been carried on in Norfolk since time immemorial. Change – any change – even a change for the better – is regretted.

Even where a change in farming methods has proved profitable, the farmer concerned does not love it. "Fancy me, a Norfolk farmer, having anything to do with things like asparagus and Brussels sprouts!" is the prevailing attitude.

A G Street, Country Calendar, 1935

***

Some misguided people think that "Norfolk" is merely a shortening of "Northfolk", but this is entirely wrong. The real derivation is "Noahfolk", showing that we are all descended in a direct line from that great navigator and explorer.

That this is so is patent from Noah's conversation with his son Japheth during an anxious moment in the Ark. (I am not for the moment able to lay my hands on the reference.)

"Japhat," he said, "ha' that mucky old dow come back yit?", to which Japheth replied: "Noo, faather, that ha'ent, not yit that ha'ent." No one could want better proof of our descent than that.

Of course, Noah thought he knew something about floods, but he ought to have been in Norwich in 1912! "We'd ha' larnt him!"

B Knyvet Wilson, Norfolk Tales and Memories, 1930

***

The story is told of a North Norfolk fisherman who came into his local pub looking drawn and miserable with his hand bandaged.

The publican asked him what had happened, and he explained that while gutting a fish he had got a bone buried in his hand , and had been unable to remove it.

The publican sent one of his customers out to the field behind the pub to fetch a large dock leaf and a cow pat. The fresh cow manure was plastered on the man's hand, which was then wrapped in the dock leaf. The patient complained of awful pain in his hand. "Never mind, drink up" he was ordered, and a pint put in front of him.

Some half an hour later the poultice was removed, and there was the white end of the cod bone sticking up. It was quite easy to remove!

Gabrielle Hatfield, Country Remedies, 1994

***

One of the definite pleasures of winter in which the Fens excel is the beauty to be found in newly-ploughed fields, or better still, a field that is still being ploughed. There is nothing dainty or pretty about this beauty.

The beauty is in the strength, weight, size and quantity of the land as well as in the sunlight reflecting on its muscular flanks. A ploughed field is like a magnificent horse – powerful and noble. You can breath, watch its sinews twitch and its flesh glisten.

As I admired a man ploughing this morning I realised what a conflict of strength there is between the machine and the soil. The shining ploughshares thrust themselves into the earth, to subdue it, but the earth rolls over and, in the end, subdues the plough. The earth survives more than a season.

Edward Storey, The Winter Fens, 1993

***

I looked in all directions, as far as I could stare over the wilderness, and away at the sea, and away at the river, but no house could I make out. There was a black barge, or some other kind of superannuated boat, not far off, high and dry on the ground, with an iron funnel sticking out of it for a chimney and smoking very cosily.

"That's not it," said I – "that ship-looking thing?" "That's it, mas'r Davy," returned Ham.

If it had been Aladdin's palace, roc's egg and all, I suppose I could not have been more charmed with the romantic idea of living in it. There was a delightful door cut in the side, and it was roofed in, and there were little windows in it; but the wonderful charm of it was, that it was a real boat.

Charles Dickens, David Copperfield, 1850

***

Norfolk is the most suspicious county in England. In Devon and Somerset men hit you on the back cordially; in Norfolk they look as though they would like to hit you over the head – till they size you up.

You see, for centuries the north folk of East Anglia was accustomed to meet stray Vikings on lonely roads who had just waded ashore from the long boats.

"Good morning, bor!" said the Viking. "Which is the way to the church?"

"What d'ye want to know for?" was the Norfolk retort.

"Well, we thought about setting fire to it!"

You will gather that Norfolk's suspicion of strangers is well grounded, and should never annoy the traveller.

H V Morton,   In Search of England, 1927

***

A cousin of mine arrived with the following amusing sidelight on the Norfolk character.

At a recent London luncheon party she found herself sitting next a distinguished American lady who had to flee the country because of threats to kidnap her daughter. She was anxiously discussing in what part of England she should buy a house and settle.

After having run through the advantages of various counties she concluded: "Of course, I did think of Norfolk, but believe me a friend of mine said: 'My dear, never go there. It's a dreadful place: I assure you no one in Norfolk ever calls till the third generation!"

Lilias Rider Haggard, Norfolk Life, 1943

EPILOGUE

Through Nelson's Burnham Thorpe to Overy Staithe, to find a thunderstorm sweeping over the salt marshes and away out across the sandbars. After lunch I cut down through the Creakes, perfect cobbled villages, with a little stream, playground of innumerable dappled ducks, chuckling over brown stones by the cottage doors, and so through Fakenham to Guist and Twyford. I came back by way of Little Snoring and Walsingham (a place reverenced throughout most of the Christian world, during the past thousand years), turned into the side roads, and climbed the slope until below on my left, lapped in green pastures, lay Binham Priory. So in the past must pilgrims travelling from the Walsingham Shrine have first seen a mightier Binham. Through the ford and up the slope again until beyond Langham the view, which always keeps one in unconscious expectancy, suddenly appears as one tops the crest. That long, lovely stretch of coastline, from Cley to Wells, lying a tranquil, many-coloured patchwork in the autumn sunshine, the Point gold-washed against lowering thundercloud and lapis sea. "This England – that has my bones!"

Norfolk Life, Lilias Rider Haggard, 1936

Most natives who have cause to leave the county are pleased enough to come home.
This was summed up admirably by the local vicar at the function I attended the other evening.
He gave thanks for "that invisible piece of elastic which keeps pinging you back to Norfolk".